Quick & Easy
LOW-SUGAR RECIPES

Quarto.com

First Published in 2024 by New Shoe Press, an imprint of The Quarto Group,
100 Cummings Center, Suite 265-D, Beverly, MA 01915, USA.
T (978) 282-9590 F (978) 283-2742

Essential, In-Demand Topics, Four-Color Design, Affordable Price

New Shoe Press publishes affordable, beautifully designed books covering evergreen, in-demand subjects. With a goal to inform and inspire readers' everyday hobbies, from cooking and gardening to wellness and health to art and crafts, New Shoe titles offer the ultimate library of purposeful, how-to guidance aimed at meeting the unique needs of each reader. Reimagined and redesigned from Quarto's best-selling backlist, New Shoe books provide practical knowledge and opportunities for all DIY enthusiasts to enrich and enjoy their lives.

Visit Quarto.com/New-Shoe-Press for a complete listing of the New Shoe Press books.

New Shoe Press titles are also available at discount for retail, wholesale, promotional, and bulk purchase. For details, contact the Special Sales Manager by email at specialsales@quarto.com or by mail at The Quarto Group, Attn: Special Sales Manager, 100 Cummings Center, Suite 265-D, Beverly, MA 01915, USA.

10 9 8 7 6 5 4 3 2 1

ISBN: 978-0-7603-9048-1
eISBN: 978-0-7603-9049-8

The content in this book was previously published in *Low Sugar, So Simple* (Fair Winds Press 2018) by Elviira Krebber.

Library of Congress Cataloging-in-Publication Data available

Photography: Kristin Teig

Printed in China

The information in this book is for educational purposes only. It is not intended to replace the advice of a physician or medical practitioner. Please see your health-care provider before beginning any new health program.

Quick & Easy

LOW-SUGAR RECIPES

Delicious Low-Carb Recipes for Crushing Cravings and Eating Clean

ELVIIRA KREBBER

NEW SHOE PRESS

Contents

Introduction

I used to be a real sugar addict. Thanks to my sweet tooth, I was overweight throughout childhood, and I was bullied at school because of it. (I was even heavier than the heaviest boys in the class!) My mom is an excellent cook, and whenever I was around, her pies, cakes, and cookies disappeared as quickly as she prepared them. When I knew she'd baked a delicious blueberry pie, I couldn't resist the temptation: I would cut one slice, then another, and another until there wasn't a crumb left! Inside, though, I was vulnerable and suffering from the constant bullying. I so desperately wanted to be thin that I started to cut calories drastically. Eventually I was diagnosed with anorexia.

After high school, though, I really lost control of my eating. I went back to eating sugar, and things got even worse. When I was studying industrial design close to the Arctic Circle, not a day would pass when I didn't indulge in a gigantic chocolate bar—and the endless darkness during the polar night exacerbated my sugar cravings. So it was no wonder that I started suffering from migraines and irritable bowel syndrome (IBS). I devoured pizzas and pastas, and poured copious amounts of sugar onto just about everything I ate. I bought cakes, muffins, candies—anything sweet—and ate them all at once. I knew it didn't do me any good, but I couldn't stop.

Later when I attended a language course in England, I enjoyed all the local "delicacies." My favorite was a super-supreme donut, a huge pastry filled with vanilla custard and coated with chocolate glaze. I gulped it down cheerfully along with a large chocolate milkshake. On the way home from school to my host family, I grabbed some humbugs—a local sweet—plus some fudge, and enjoyed them while walking. On my class trip to France, I bought a 14-ounce (400 g) bar of Toblerone and ate it in a single day. On the last day of the course, I celebrated by buying a huge carrot cake, which I divided with my roommate. (At least I didn't gobble it up all by myself, for a change!)

All that sugar made me feel miserable. Not only did I have physical ailments, but I was also suffering from depression, anxiety, and panic attacks. I had anorexia in my past, and now I developed another type of eating disorder: bulimia. I was frightened to death of vomiting, so I popped laxative pills like candies—dozens and dozens per day. Sitting in agony on the toilet didn't bother me much, as long as I got rid of the junk I'd eaten as quickly as possible.

Soon my condition worsened. I started suffering from unexplained stomach pains. In 1999, my colon was removed, and for a year after that I felt wonderful. However, the IBS symptoms came back, along with even worse pain. My weight plummeted until my BMI was only 12.7. I had arrhythmia, terrible stomach pains, and brain fog. No doctor could give me a diagnosis. The lab results all came back fine, but I felt like I was dying.

So I had no other choice but to take control of my health. I started to study nutrition, and soon I learned how destructive sugar is. I cut it out of my diet—and cereals, too, because I'd heard lots of success stories from people who regained their health by omitting gluten from their diets. (Little did I know at that point that cereals were, in practice, sugar. If that is a surprise to you, too, don't worry: I'll explain in the chapters that follow.)

As I quit sugar, I added more fat to my diet. It took a long time to understand how vital fat is to health—natural fat, that is. My brain fog finally disappeared after I started consuming butter and other natural fats.

After I made these changes—quitting sugar and starch, and adding more fat to my diet—I started getting better. Much, much better. My weight normalized, and I was no longer bulimic; I suffered fewer migraines;

Note to the Reader

- All eggs used are U.S. size large, and should be organic and free-range whenever possible, because these contain more omega-3 fats and other nutrients. (Plus, they taste better!)

- Be sure to use the freshest ingredients and those of the best quality. Organic, non-GMO vegetables are best. As for meat and dairy products, choose those from animals fed with a species-specific diet. (For example, choose dairy and beef products that come from grass-fed cows.)

- Milk and cream should be organic, if possible, and free from food additives.

- All citrus fruits (especially lemons) should be organic and unwaxed.

- Baking powder should be aluminum-free. Cinnamon should be Ceylon cinnamon, or true cinnamon—not the more common cassia or Chinese cinnamon, which is toxic to the liver.

and my anxiety and panic attacks disappeared. I wasn't depressed anymore. And my stomach finally felt great! No more IBS, no more bloating; all that crippling pain had disappeared. Now I enjoyed a flat tummy. I had six-pack abs without even trying. My entire body composition was ripped and muscular in comparison to the way it looked before. When I ate sugar—even when I wasn't overweight—I had a flabby stomach, enormous thighs, and a round face. Now my body looked toned and fit, even though I didn't do any sports.

With my new lifestyle, though, I noticed that it wasn't easy to find truly healthy recipes. In fact, most of the sugar-free recipes I came across didn't seem to be sugar-free at all. They contained dried fruit, syrups such as agave or rice syrup, or starches. Many of them had artificial sweeteners, too. I'd found healthy, sugar-free natural sweeteners myself, but couldn't find recipes for them. So I had to create everything from scratch. I developed recipes for breads, desserts, breakfasts, main courses, side dishes, and more—all with a minimal number of ingredients and steps, because I was busy and impatient.

Then in 2012, I established my *Low-Carb, So Simple* blog to help people in the same situation as I was— seeking easy, healthy recipes after switching to a low-sugar lifestyle. Five years later, I'm delighted to have more than 600,000 Facebook followers and hundreds of thousands of blog readers. There seems to be a huge demand for easy, truly healthy low-sugar recipes, and this is very understandable. With the current biased dietary guidelines and a food industry that spends billions on marketing its junk, people are getting sick, both literally and figuratively. They have to discover the truth behind these lies by themselves. Like parrots, doctors and dietitians still adhere to the low-fat religion, emphasizing the importance of "healthy" whole grains and fruit, not realizing that these substances actually make people sick.

Today we've finally started to understand that fat is your friend while sugar is the thing making you sick. Knowing that, we can move toward perfect health by savoring delicious, natural, clean food without sugar and starch. This book will show you how to do just that. Enjoy!

CHAPTER 1

Basics & Pantry Staples

It's normal to feel overwhelmed when you're starting a low-sugar lifestyle, and you might have a lot of questions about it. What can you eat, and what's off-limits? Which ingredients should you choose? How do you prepare low-sugar food that's both nutritious and delicious?

Well, this chapter is here to help. It's full of low-sugar recipes for the staples you'll be using again and again, so that you'll always have healthy ingredients on hand, and won't have to reach for sugar-laden processed stuff in a pinch. (Plus, the homemade versions taste better.)

So, whether you're looking for sugar-free ketchup (a guaranteed kid-pleaser!), easy-to-make mayo, guilt-free jams and marmalades, or fluffy, sliceable starch-free bread, you're sure to find inspiration in the pages that follow.

Low-Sugar Sweet and Sour Sauce

Commercial sweet and sour sauce easily contains more than 30 percent sugar, but this flavorful, homemade version has ten times less! Better yet, this exceptionally simple and seriously good condiment is ready in no time: Just mix all the ingredients together and heat until thick. Use it as a wok sauce for Asian-style dishes, in the Easy Breakfast Burrito on page 51, or serve it as a condiment with chicken or vegetable dishes. It also makes a great dip for starch-free crackers and raw vegetables.

⅔ cup (160 ml) water

½ cup (65 g) powdered erythritol

3 tablespoons (45 ml) rice vinegar

3 tablespoons (48 g) unsweetened tomato paste

1½ tablespoons (25 ml) naturally fermented gluten-free soy sauce, such as tamari

15 drops liquid stevia, or to taste

¼ teaspoon unrefined sea salt or Himalayan salt, or to taste

½ teaspoon xanthan gum

—
Yield: about 1¾ cups (410 ml)

Place the water, erythritol, vinegar, tomato paste, soy sauce, stevia, and salt in a small saucepan and whisk well. Sprinkle in the xanthan while constantly whisking. Place the saucepan over a high heat, constantly mixing. When the mixture starts to thicken—and before it begins to boil—remove it from the heat. Let cool to room temperature before refrigerating. Store in an airtight container in the fridge. The sauce tastes best the following day, after the flavors have had time to combine. Use within two weeks.

NUTRITION INFO

IN TOTAL:

3.3 G PROTEIN	
0.4 G FAT	
12.2 G NET CARBS	
66 KCAL	

PER TABLESPOON (15 ML):

0.1 G PROTEIN	
TRACE FAT	
0.5 G NET CARBS	
3 KCAL	

TIP:

If you don't have rice vinegar, use raw apple cider vinegar or another mild-tasting vinegar instead.

Five-Ingredient Sugar-Free Ketchup

This is every parent's dream: super-healthy, sugar-free ketchup! Made with an erythritol-based brown sugar substitute that is almost noncaloric, it's a healthy condiment that's delicious for dipping low-carb rutabaga or turnip fries, or the Easy Broccoli "Tater Tots" on page 104. Remember that placing the ketchup mixture over a higher heat causes it to thicken faster—but it does splatter easily, so take care and keep a lid handy while cooking.

2 cups (450 g) unsweetened tomato sauce

¼ cup (40 g) erythritol-based brown sugar substitute

2 tablespoons (28 ml) raw apple cider vinegar

⅛ teaspoon Ceylon cinnamon

Pinch of cayenne pepper

—
Yield: about 2 cups (450 g)

Place all the ingredients in a medium saucepan over a high heat and bring to a boil. Reduce the heat to medium and boil, uncovered, until the ketchup has reached the desired consistency (about 30 minutes), stirring every 5 minutes. As the ketchup thickens, it may splatter, so be careful. If so, reduce the heat and cover the saucepan with a lid until the splattering stops. Let cool to room temperature before refrigerating. Store in an airtight container in the fridge, and use within one week.

NUTRITION INFO

IN TOTAL:

5.9 G PROTEIN

TRACE FAT

20.1 G NET CARBS

121 KCAL

PER TABLESPOON (14 G):

0.2 G PROTEIN

TRACE FAT

0.7 G NET CARBS

4 KCAL

No-Sugar Teriyaki Sauce

Traditional Japanese teriyaki sauce is sweet and tangy, but commercial versions often contain a huge amount of sugar, which can be responsible for as much one-third of their total calorie count. This guilt-free version, however, has no added sugar. Instead, it gets its sweetness from an erythritol-based brown sugar substitute, which is almost calorie-free. It's easy to adjust the level of sweetness to your taste.

½ cup (120 ml) naturally fermented gluten-free soy sauce, such as tamari

⅓ cup (53 g) erythritol-based brown sugar substitute

¼ cup (60 ml) dry sherry

¼ cup (60 ml) rice vinegar

1 teaspoon ground ginger

¼ teaspoon garlic powder

—
Yield: about 1 cup (240 ml)

Place all ingredients in a small saucepan and bring to a boil over a high heat, mixing constantly. Once boiling, remove from the heat and let cool to room temperature. Use it just like traditional teriyaki sauce—to make teriyaki chicken, for example, or the Terrific Teriyaki Pork Sandwich on page 72.

NOTE:

If you prefer a thicker sauce, sprinkle ½ teaspoon xanthan gum or glucomannan into the mixture before heating. Whisk carefully when adding the thickener to prevent lumps.

NUTRITION INFO

IN TOTAL:

12.3 G PROTEIN

0.3 G FAT

8.8 G NET CARBS

154 KCAL

PER TABLESPOON (15 ML):

0.6 G PROTEIN

TRACE FAT

0.5 G NET CARBS

8 KCAL

TIP:

If you want to use fresh ingredients, replace the garlic powder with 1 minced garlic clove and replace the ground ginger with 1 tablespoon (8 g) of grated ginger root.

Foolproof One-Minute Mayo

Think it's hard to make homemade mayonnaise? Think again. This is the quickest, easiest way to prepare mayonnaise, ever, and it's healthy as well because it calls for light olive oil instead of unhealthy, omega-6-filled canola or sunflower oil. (Light olive oil is more neutral-tasting than extra-virgin, which might be too strong for mayonnaise.) This simple mayo is used in lots of recipes in this book, so be sure to keep a batch on hand. (Note that this recipe contains raw egg.)

1 very fresh egg

2 teaspoons unsweetened mustard (such as Dijon)

⅛ teaspoon ground white pepper

¼ teaspoon unrefined sea salt or Himalayan salt, or to taste

2 teaspoons raw apple cider vinegar

¾ cup (180 ml) extra-light olive oil

—
Yield: about 1 cup (225 g)

Place the egg, mustard, white pepper, salt, and vinegar into a deep, narrow blending jar. Then insert an immersion blender into the jar so that it reaches the bottom.

Now pour in the olive oil. Don't lift the immersion blender or turn it on yet: Let it stand in the bottom of the jar, covering the egg and the other ingredients.

Start blending on the highest speed. Blend until the oil is completely incorporated and the mayonnaise is smooth. (You can lift the blender very slowly at the end of the process to make sure all the oil is incorporated.) This phase shouldn't take longer than a minute. Store the finished mayonnaise in the fridge for up to two days.

NUTRITION INFO

IN TOTAL:

8.4 G PROTEIN

225.2 G FAT

0.7 G NET CARBS

2064 KCAL

PER TABLESPOON (14 G):

0.4 G PROTEIN

11.3 G FAT

TRACE NET CARBS

103 KCAL

Fantastic French Dressing

Here's another classic low-carb dressing that combines great taste and good fats. And its sharp yet sophisticated flavor is a perfect match for the Greek Salad with Chicken and Strawberries on page 66, or similarly fruity-yet-savory salads. If you prefer your dressing on the sweet side, add a couple of drops of liquid stevia to the mix.

1 tablespoon (15 ml) freshly squeezed lemon juice

⅓ cup (80 ml) extra-virgin olive oil

¼ teaspoon mustard powder

1 garlic clove, crushed

Pinch unrefined sea salt or Himalayan salt

—
Yield: about 6 tablespoons (95 ml)

Place all the ingredients in a small jar with a tight-fitting lid. Close the lid tightly and shake vigorously until the mixture is smooth. For best results, let the flavors mingle for a few hours before serving.

Store in the fridge and bring to room temperature 30 minutes before use. Shake well before serving.

NUTRITION INFO

IN TOTAL:

0.5 G PROTEIN	
73.5 G FAT	
0.8 G NET CARBS	
666 KCAL	

PER TABLESPOON (16 ML):

0.1 G PROTEIN	
12.2 G FAT	
0.1 G NET CARBS	
111 KCAL	

Quick Raspberry Vinaigrette

This flavorful, easy-to-make vinaigrette adds a dash of elegance to just about any salad, and it's also a delicious way to add extra vitamins and healthy fats to your diet—minus the nasty sugar and its harmful effects, of course. Use a high-speed blender to break up the gritty seeds and to achieve a smooth, rich result. Feel free to experiment with other berries here, too, such as strawberries and blueberries.

¼ **cup (25 g) fresh raspberries, or thawed frozen raspberries**

2 tablespoons (28 ml) raw apple cider vinegar

6 tablespoons (90 ml) extra-virgin olive oil

5 drops liquid stevia, or to taste

¼ **teaspoon unrefined sea salt or Himalayan salt, or to taste**

—
Yield: about ⅔ cup (160 ml)

Simply place all the ingredients in a high-speed blender and blend until smooth. Serve immediately, or store in an airtight container in the fridge and bring to room temperature 30 minutes before use. Shake well before serving.

NOTE:

To make this recipe even simpler, make a batch of the Easy Sugar-Free Strawberry Jam recipe on page 21 ahead of time, replacing the strawberries with raspberries. Then, to make this vinaigrette, just replace the raspberries and stevia with 2 tablespoons (30 g) of the jam.

NUTRITION INFO

IN TOTAL:

0.4 G PROTEIN	
82.3 G FAT	
1.6 G NET CARBS	
749 KCAL	

PER TABLESPOON (15 ML):

TRACE PROTEIN	
8.2 G FAT	
0.2 G NET CARBS	
75 KCAL	

Five-Ingredient Sugar-Free Chocolate Hazelnut Spread

Commercial chocolate hazelnut spreads contain both a good deal of sugar and processed vegetable oils, which are infamous for their inflammation-inflicting omega-6 content. But this healthy, homemade option uses only natural sweeteners and real butter, which is far heart healthier. Smear it on a slice of Easy Fluffy Bread (page 24) for a quick, light breakfast or snack.

¾ cup (85 g) crushed toasted hazelnuts

¼ cup (2 ounces or 60 g) unsalted grass-fed butter, softened

1 tablespoon (7 g) unsweetened dark cocoa powder

3 tablespoons (24 g) powdered erythritol or other preferred sweetener, or to taste

2 tablespoons (28 ml) extra-light olive oil

½ teaspoon vanilla extract (optional)

—
Yield: about ¾ cup (195 g)

Combine all the ingredients in a high-speed blender and blend until a smooth paste is formed. Add more sweetener if needed, then blend well again. Store in an airtight container in the fridge and bring to room temperature 30 minutes before use. Use within one week.

NUTRITION INFO

IN TOTAL:

15.4 G PROTEIN

130.1 G FAT

5.5 G NET CARBS

1260 KCAL

PER TABLESPOON (16 G):

1.1 G PROTEIN

9.3 G FAT

0.4 G NET CARBS

90 KCAL

Simple and Succulent Satay Sauce

Full of richness and exotic flavor, this Thai-style satay sauce is ready in mere minutes. Enjoy it warm with chicken, fish, or vegetable dishes, and don't forget to add chopped salted peanuts before serving: They enhance the flavor and texture even more. If you prefer a thicker sauce, increase the amount of peanut butter; if you prefer a thinner sauce, increase the coconut milk.

1 cup (240 ml) coconut milk

⅔ cup (160 g) crunchy unsweetened peanut butter

1½ tablespoons (23 g) sugar-free Thai red curry paste

1 to 2 tablespoons (15 to 28 ml) fish sauce

10 drops liquid stevia, or to taste

¼ cup (30 g) chopped salted peanuts, to serve

—

Yield: about 2 cups (480 ml)

Combine all the ingredients in a small saucepan and place over high heat, stirring constantly. When the mixture is hot and smooth, remove it from the heat. Let cool slightly and serve warm, sprinkled with chopped peanuts.

NUTRITION INFO

IN TOTAL:

57.0 G PROTEIN

150.5 G FAT

30.4 G NET CARBS

1704 KCAL

PER ¼ CUP (60 ML):

7.1 G PROTEIN

18.8 G FAT

3.8 G NET CARBS

213 KCAL

TIP:

For a fruitier-tasting sauce, replace the stevia with 2 tablespoons (30 g) of Five-Ingredient Sugar-Free Ketchup (page 10).

Low-Sugar Orange Marmalade

Traditional orange marmalade is terribly high in sugar—but now you can enjoy all that fresh, succulent flavor without sugar and its harmful effects. Plus, this marmalade has a smooth texture, which makes it easily spreadable (and more kid-friendly). Discarding the white pith of the orange before cooking guarantees a perfectly fruity marmalade without a hint of bitterness, and long, slow cooking ensures naturally deep, sweet flavors.

2 oranges

1 cup (240 ml) plus ¼ cup (60 ml) water divided

1 cup (130 g) powdered erythritol

40 drops orange-flavored stevia

2 teaspoons gelatin powder

2 drops 100 percent orange essential oil

—
Yield: about 2½ cups (750 g)

NUTRITION INFO

IN TOTAL:

9.7 G PROTEIN

0.4 G FAT

31.5 G NET CARBS

199 KCAL

PER ¼ CUP (60 G):

1.0 G PROTEIN

TRACE FAT

3.2 G NET CARBS

20 KCAL

PER TABLESPOON (20 G):

0.2 G PROTEIN

TRACE FAT

0.8 G NET CARBS

5 KCAL

Wash the oranges and pat them dry. Finely grate the peel from 1 orange and place it in a medium saucepan. (Be sure to grate the orange part of the peel only and leave out the white pith: it's very bitter.)

Peel both oranges. Discard the peels and seeds and use only the flesh. Remove as much of the white pith as possible. Chop the flesh into ½-inch (1.3 cm) chunks. Add these to the saucepan, along with 1 cup (240 ml) of the water, the powdered erythritol, and the orange stevia. Mix well and bring to a boil over a high heat. Once boiling, reduce the heat to low. Cover, and let the mixture simmer for 3 hours.

When the mixture has simmered for close to 3 hours, pour the remaining ¼ cup (60 ml) water into a small cup. Sprinkle the gelatin powder on top. Let the gelatin soak and thicken for 5 minutes, then add it to the hot orange mixture and mix well until completely dissolved. Add the orange essential oil and mix again. Pour the hot marmalade into sterilized glass jars or a ceramic container. Let cool to room temperature, then refrigerate overnight. The marmalade will set in the fridge. Store in the fridge and consume within two weeks.

Easy Sugar-Free Strawberry Jam

You won't believe how easy it is to make homemade sugar-free strawberry jam. And you can tailor it to your taste, too: Cooking the mixture for less time yields a chunkier jam, while longer cooking results in a smoother texture and a sweeter flavor. Use this summery jam to dress up your breakfast yogurt or to accompany a sugar-free cheesecake, or slather it on a slice of starch-free peanut butter bread to make a healthy PB&J sandwich.

1 pound (450 g) fresh strawberries, or thawed frozen strawberries

¼ cup (32 g) powdered erythritol

40 drops liquid vanilla stevia, or to taste

2 pinches xanthan gum

—
Yield: about 1½ cups (350 g)

NUTRITION INFO

IN TOTAL:

2.3 G PROTEIN	
0.9 G FAT	
38.1 G NET CARBS	
172 KCAL	

PER TABLESPOON (15 G):

0.1 G PROTEIN	
TRACE FAT	
1.4 G NET CARBS	
6 KCAL	

Combine the strawberries, erythritol, and vanilla stevia in a large saucepan. Place over a high heat, stirring constantly (and scraping the bottom of the saucepan as you stir). When the mixture begins to steam, reduce the heat to low. Cook for 15 to 20 minutes, or until the mixture has reached the desired consistency. (Feel free to leave it as chunky as you like.) Mix constantly during cooking, crushing and breaking the strawberries with the back and sides of the mixing spoon.

Sprinkle in the xanthan gum little by little on top of the mixture, stirring all the time. (If you like, you can sift in the xanthan gum through a tea strainer to prevent lumps.) Continue mixing and let the jam simmer for 2 to 3 minutes before removing from the heat. Cover with a lid and let the jam cool completely. Store it in an airtight container in the fridge and consume within one week. You can also freeze the jam for up to two months, or preserve it for longer in sterilized glass jars.

Three-Ingredient Sugar-Free Caramel Glaze

Great news: It's possible to make a healthy, sugar-free caramel glaze with just three natural ingredients. Sound too good to be true? Well, it's not! In fact, you can make caramel using just two ingredients—heavy cream and erythritol—but the salted butter enhances its flavor and produces a perfectly glossy sauce. And the longer you cook it, the thicker your sauce will be. Try topping your favorite low-sugar desserts with this luscious treat.

1½ cups (350 ml) heavy cream

3 tablespoons (30 g) erythritol-based brown sugar substitute

1 tablespoon (14 g) salted grass-fed butter

—

Yield: about 1 cup (240 ml)

Place the heavy cream and the sweetener in a medium saucepan and bring to a boil over a medium-high heat, stirring constantly. Reduce the heat to medium, then simmer uncovered until thick, about 15 minutes, stirring all the time. You'll know the sauce is ready when you can see the bottom of the saucepan as you whisk it. Be sure to watch the mixture constantly during cooking; it can boil over in seconds. Reduce the heat if the mixture is about to spill.

When the caramel is thick, remove from the heat. Add the butter and mix well, until the butter is melted and is completely incorporated into the mixture.

Cover and let it cool down. Use as glaze or sauce immediately, or store in the fridge in an airtight container and consume within three days.

NUTRITION INFO

IN TOTAL:	
7.4 G PROTEIN	
138.2 G FAT	
11.7 G NET CARBS	
1319 KCAL	
PER TABLESPOON (15 ML):	
0.5 G PROTEIN	
8.6 G FAT	
0.7 G NET CARBS	
82 KCAL	

TIP:

Be extremely careful with the boiling cream, as it boils over very easily. Using a larger saucepan helps prevent this, and also allows you to use a higher heat, which, in turn, reduces cooking time.

Homemade Sugar-Free Maple Syrup

There's no need to skimp on this delicious condiment: You can happily drown your starch-free pancakes and waffles in it without worrying about the harmful sugar load that's part and parcel of traditional maple syrup. And it tastes, looks, and feels just like the real thing! I use Frontier Natural Products maple flavor for this recipe, so if you use another type of maple flavor, be sure to adjust the amount accordingly.

1½ cups (350 ml) water

¾ cup (120 g) erythritol-based brown sugar substitute

½ teaspoon glucomannan

1 teaspoon sugar-free maple flavoring, or to taste

—

Yield: about 2 cups (475 ml)

Combine the water and the sweetener in a small saucepan and bring to a rolling boil over high heat. Mix a couple of times while heating.

Remove the saucepan from the heat and, very carefully, sprinkle in the glucomannan while whisking vigorously to prevent lumps. Add the maple flavoring and mix well again. Adjust the taste by adding more sweetener or maple flavoring, if necessary. Let cool to room temperature. The syrup will thicken during cooling. Pour the syrup into a glass bottle and store in the fridge for up to two weeks.

TIP:
Glucomannan is the best thickener to use here because it produces the smoothest, most neutral-tasting result.

NUTRITION INFO

IN TOTAL:

0.1 G PROTEIN	
TRACE FAT	
3.5 G NET CARBS	
10 KCAL	

PER TABLESPOON (15 ML):

TRACE PROTEIN	
TRACE FAT	
0.1 G NET CARBS	
0 KCAL	

NOTE:

This "maple syrup" is intentionally less sweet than regular maple syrup, to help wean you off the unnaturally sweet taste. However, if you'd like to make it sweeter, use 1 cup (240 ml) erythritol-based brown sugar substitute.

Easy Fluffy Bread

In 2012, I posted my first fluffy bread recipe on my blog. Since then, I've made several improvements to the recipe, this one being the latest—and absolute best!—version. Its texture is fabulously light and fluffy, but it holds together extremely well, so slice it as thinly as you like.

¼ cup (30 g) unflavored egg white protein powder

¼ cup (20 g) unflavored grass-fed whey protein powder

1 tablespoon (9 g) psyllium husk powder

2 teaspoons baking powder

4 eggs, separated

½ cup (120 g) unsweetened cashew butter

½ cup (120 ml) unsweetened almond milk

1 teaspoon unrefined sea salt (optional)

5 drops liquid stevia, or to taste (optional)

—

Yield: 1 loaf

Preheat the oven to 350°F (175°C). Combine the egg white protein, whey protein, psyllium husk powder, and baking powder in a small bowl. Mix well to break up any lumps.

In a separate bowl, beat the egg whites until stiff peaks form.

Combine the cashew butter and egg yolks in a large bowl and beat until well combined. Then add the almond milk and salt and stevia, if using, and beat again. Add the dry ingredients to the wet, and mix well. Fold in the egg whites and mix gently with a rubber spatula until smooth. Pour the mixture into a 9 × 5-inch (23 × 13 cm) silicone loaf pan.

Bake in the preheated oven for 45 minutes, or until a toothpick inserted in the center of the loaf comes out clean. Remove from the pan, let cool completely, and serve.

NUTRITION INFO

IN TOTAL:

84.3 G PROTEIN	
95.9 G FAT	
22.6 G NET CARBS	
1293 KCAL	

PER SLICE,
IF 12 SLICES IN TOTAL:

7.0 G PROTEIN	
8.0 G FAT	
1.9 G NET CARBS	
108 KCAL	

PER SLICE,
IF 24 SLICES IN TOTAL:

3.5 G PROTEIN	
4.0 G FAT	
0.9 G NET CARBS	
54 KCAL	

TIP:

For even lower sugar content, replace the cashew butter with macadamia nut butter.

Low-Sugar Cinnamon Raisin Bread

Raisins are relatively high in natural sugars—but this delicious Cinnamon Raisin Bread isn't. What's the secret? Chopping the raisins into tiny pieces, which yields plenty of flavor with minimal sugar. And if you add extra cinnamon and sweetener, you'll be able to reduce the quantity of raisins even further.

¾ cup (90 g) coconut flour

⅓ cup (45 g) finely chopped raisins

¼ cup (20 g) vanilla-flavored grass-fed whey protein powder

3 tablespoons (27 g) psyllium husk powder

2 teaspoons baking powder

2 teaspoons Ceylon cinnamon

¼ teaspoon unrefined sea salt or Himalayan salt

6 eggs

1 cup (240 ml) unsweetened almond milk

25 drops liquid stevia

—
Yield: 1 loaf

Preheat the oven to 350°F (175°C). Place all the dry ingredients in a medium bowl. Mix well, making sure there are no lumps.

Place the eggs, almond milk, and stevia in another medium bowl and whisk well. Add the dry ingredients to the wet, then mix with an electric mixer until smooth. Transfer the batter to a 9 × 5-inch (23 × 13 cm) silicone loaf pan. Use a rubber spatula to form it into a loaf shape. Bake for 60 minutes, or until a toothpick inserted in the center of the loaf comes out dry. Remove from the pan, let cool completely, and serve.

NUTRITION INFO

IN TOTAL:	
81.5 G PROTEIN	
58.7 G FAT	
55.6 G NET CARBS	
1079 KCAL	
PER SLICE, IF 24 SLICES IN TOTAL:	
3.4 G PROTEIN	
2.4 G FAT	
2.3 G NET CARBS	
45 KCAL	

TIP:

For variation, add ¼ cup (75 g) Low-Sugar Orange Marmalade (page 19) to the wet ingredients.

Two-Minute Mile-High English Muffin in a Mug

A few basic ingredients and a couple of minutes are all you need to whip up a low-sugar English muffin that's the perfect vehicle for just about any kind of topping, such as salad, meat, eggs, cheese, or veggies. Or, for an elegant-yet-filling weekend treat, try filling it with lox, cream cheese, dill, and red onion. You won't even miss the bagel!

Softened butter (for greasing the mug)

¼ cup (30 g) almond flour

1 teaspoon psyllium husk powder

¼ teaspoon aluminum-free baking powder

1 pinch unrefined sea salt or Himalayan salt, or to taste

1 egg

1 tablespoon (15 ml) soda water (or any sparkling water)

—

Yield: 1 serving

Grease a microwave-safe cup with softened butter. (The higher and narrower the cup, the better the muffin will rise.)

Combine the almond flour, psyllium husk powder, baking powder, and salt in a small bowl, taking care to break up any lumps. Add the egg and mix well with a spoon. Add the carbonated water and mix well again. Spoon the batter into the greased cup, then microwave on high for 2 minutes. (Check the muffin after 1 minute and adjust the total cooking time according to your microwave oven.)

Remove the muffin from the cup, let cool slightly, slice, and enjoy warm with your favorite toppings, or toast it, if you like.

NUTRITION INFO

IN TOTAL:

15.0 G PROTEIN

22.3 G FAT

2.5 G NET CARBS

270 KCAL

Sugar-Free, Starch-Free Pie Crust

Traditional pie crust is filled with starch—mainly wheat flour—which means it's hardly a healthy choice. Never fear, though: It's not difficult to make a thin, flaky starch-free pastry that's perfect for sweet and savory pies alike. If you're using this crust to make a sweet pie, add 2 tablespoons (16 g) of powdered erythritol to the dry ingredients, or a couple of drops liquid stevia to the wet ingredients.

½ cup (60 g) almond flour

¼ cup (30 g) coconut flour

2 tablespoons (18 g) psyllium husk powder

1 teaspoon aluminum-free baking powder

Pinch unrefined sea salt or Himalayan salt

3 eggs

2 tablespoons (30 ml) light olive oil

—
Yield: 1 pie crust

Preheat the oven to 350°F (175°C). Place the dry ingredients in a small bowl and mix them well to break up any lumps.

Place the eggs and olive oil into a medium bowl. Gradually add the dry ingredients, whisking constantly to prevent lumps. (The dough will be very sturdy, and will thicken almost immediately after adding the dry ingredients.) Press the dough evenly into the bottom and sides of a 10-inch (25 cm) pie pan. Prick the dough all over with a fork to prevent blistering, and prebake the crust for 15 minutes before adding the filling of your choice.

NUTRITION INFO

IN TOTAL:

41.7 G PROTEIN	
79.0 G FAT	
13.5 G NET CARBS	
932 KCAL	

PER SLICE, IF 8 SLICES IN TOTAL:

5.2 G PROTEIN	
9.9 G FAT	
1.7 G NET CARBS	
117 KCAL	

PER SLICE, IF 12 SLICES IN TOTAL:

3.5 G PROTEIN	
6.6 G FAT	
1.1 G NET CARBS	
78 KCAL	

Vegan Sugar-Free, Starch-Free Pie Crust

If you're vegan, you know that creating low-carb desserts can be a bit of an extra challenge. But here's some good news: You don't need egg to make a perfect pie crust. And this recipe is proof. Like its nonvegan counterpart (opposite page), it calls for just a few simple ingredients, and it can be used to make sweet and savory pies that are sure to impress your guests.

2 cups (230 g) almond flour

2 tablespoons (18 g) psyllium husk powder

½ teaspoon unrefined sea salt or Himalayan salt, or to taste

1 teaspoon aluminum-free baking powder

⅓ cup (80 ml) extra-light olive oil

¼ cup (60 ml) water

—
Yield: 1 pie crust

Preheat the oven to 350°F (175°C). Place the almond flour, psyllium husk powder, salt, and baking powder in a small bowl. Mix well to break up any lumps. Add the olive oil and water. Use clean hands to mix and knead until a stiff dough forms. Press the dough evenly into the bottom and the sides of a 10-inch (25 cm) pie pan. Prick the dough all over with a fork to prevent blistering. Prebake the crust for 10 minutes before adding the filling of your choice.

NUTRITION INFO

IN TOTAL:

44.0 G PROTEIN

174.2 G FAT

20.1 G NET CARBS

1824 KCAL

PER SLICE, IF 8 SLICES IN TOTAL:

5.5 G PROTEIN

21.8 G FAT

2.5 G NET CARBS

228 KCAL

PER SLICE, IF 12 SLICES IN TOTAL:

3.7 G PROTEIN

14.5 G FAT

1.7 G NET CARBS

152 KCAL

Single-Serve Tortilla

Is there anything quite as handy and versatile as a tortilla? It can become a burrito, a quesadilla, or a lunchtime wrap—and when it's baked, it's the perfect foundation for a plate of nachos (see the variation, below). And this starch-free version is a cinch to make. Because it has a neutral taste, it's perfect for desserts and sweet snacks, too.

2 teaspoons coconut flour

1 teaspoon psyllium husk powder

Pinch unrefined sea salt or Himalayan salt

1 egg

2 teaspoons unsweetened almond milk

—
Yield: 1 serving

TIP:

You can use almond flour instead of coconut flour, if you like. Just omit the coconut flour and add 2 tablespoons (15 g) of almond flour to the dry ingredients and then follow the recipe directions.

Combine the coconut flour, psyllium husk powder, and salt in a small bowl and mix well until combined. Add the egg and the almond milk and stir with a spoon until smooth.

Pour the mixture onto an 8-inch (20 cm) microwave-safe plate. Tilt the plate to thinly spread the batter as evenly as possible. Heat on high for 1 minute and 45 seconds, or until done. Adjust the time according to your microwave oven, but don't overbake: The tortilla will be dry if baked too long. Use a spatula or cheese slicer to remove the tortilla from the plate. Let cool and serve.

VARIATION: To make nachos: Add 1 teaspoon extra-light olive oil to the batter and omit the almond milk. Bake the tortilla for 3 minutes, turning it over after each minute. Let cool completely. Once cooled, the tortilla will be crispy and easy to break into pieces.

NUTRITION INFO

IN TOTAL:

8.5 G PROTEIN	
6.8 G FAT	
1.0 G NET CARBS	
100 KCAL	

NOTE:

For extra flavor and variety, add ½ teaspoon dried herbs or 1 teaspoon dried tomato powder to the dry ingredients.

Super-Healthy Waffles (or Pancakes)

While waffles are often thought of as breakfast food in the United States, in Europe they are eaten at every meal. You can top waffles with berries for breakfast, cream cheese and mixed greens for lunch, and hearty stews for a comforting dinner. With jam and whipped cream they are a very popular dessert. Waffles and pancakes make great substitutes to traditional high-carb options such as bread, croissants, and noodles; thus, they serve as a great basic recipe in your low-sugar cooking repertoire.

½ cup (60 g) coconut flour

¼ cup (20 g) vanilla-flavored grass-fed whey protein

1 tablespoon (7 g) milled chia seeds

2 teaspoons aluminum-free baking powder

Pinch unrefined sea salt or Himalayan salt

6 eggs

½ cup (120 ml) unsweetened almond milk

20 drops vanilla stevia

—
Yield: 6 to 8 pancakes

Place the dry ingredients in a small bowl and mix well. Place the eggs, almond milk, and stevia in a medium bowl and whisk until smooth. Gradually add the dry ingredients to the wet, stirring constantly. When completely combined, let the mixture stand for 10 minutes to thicken.

Use the batter to make waffles in your waffle maker according to the manufacturer's instructions. (Use butter for greasing the waffle maker.) To make pancakes, fry pancakes in a small skillet on medium-low heat in an ample amount of butter. Store leftover pancakes or waffles in an airtight container in the fridge and consume within one day.

NUTRITION INFO

IN TOTAL:	
72.0 G PROTEIN	
52.7 G FAT	
17.3 G NET CARBS	
833 KCAL	
PER SERVING, IF 6 SERVINGS IN TOTAL:	
12.0 G PROTEIN	
8.8 G FAT	
2.9 G NET CARBS	
139 KCAL	
PER SERVING, IF 8 SERVINGS IN TOTAL:	
9.0 G PROTEIN	
6.6 G FAT	
2.2 G NET CARBS	
104 KCAL	

TIP:

For dairy-free waffles or pancakes, replace the whey protein with rice protein, and use butter-flavored coconut oil or light olive oil for frying.

CHAPTER 2

Breakfast

When your body doesn't have to combat high insulin and blood sugar levels, you'll have lots more energy for your daily tasks. So why not start your day with a delicious, nutritious, sugar-free breakfast? The recipes in this chapter are designed to keep you satisfied for hours—until lunchtime, and then some.

Luscious Key Lime Pie Smoothie with a Secret Ingredient

If you love Key lime pie, I've got great news for you: You can have it for breakfast. This healthy green smoothie is packed with good-for-you ingredients—and don't worry if you can't find Key limes. It's just as good when it's made with regular ones. And can you guess the secret ingredient? It's one of the all-time best superfoods: sprouts. (Just don't tell your kids!)

1 cup (240 ml) unsweetened almond milk

½ cup (115 g) plain full-fat Greek or Turkish yogurt

⅓ cup (43 g) powdered erythritol

Zest of 1 small lime or zest of three Key limes

1½ tablespoons (22 ml) freshly squeezed lime juice

1 cup (50 g) well-rinsed and drained sprouts (broccoli, alfalfa, etc.), tightly packed

½ teaspoon glucomannan or xanthan gum, for thickening (optional)

—
Yield: 1 serving

Simply place all ingredients in a high-speed blender and blend until smooth. If you use xanthan gum, be sure to sprinkle it on top of the mixture before blending to prevent lumping.

VARIATION: Add 2 peeled and pitted ripe Hass avocados for a delicious Key Lime Pie Pudding! Divide the mixture between serving bowls and enjoy with a spoon.

NUTRITION INFO

IN TOTAL:

6.7 G PROTEIN

14.8 G FAT

8.7 G NET CARBS

209 KCAL

Joyful Chocolate Almond Smoothie

This guilt-free smoothie won't spike your blood sugar levels like pastries or sugary candy bars will, making it a delicious, no-cheat start to the morning, and its carefully chosen ingredients will nourish and satisfy both body and mind. (Think of it as brain food!) Plus, this smoothie is vegan and dairy-free, which means it's the ideal start to your day if you don't tolerate dairy.

1 cup (240 ml) unsweetened almond milk

¼ cup (60 g) unsweetened almond butter

2 tablespoons (15 g) unsweetened dark cocoa powder

1 tablespoon (14 g) extra-virgin coconut oil

3 tablespoons (24 g) powdered erythritol

1 teaspoon vanilla extract

—
Yield: 1 serving

Simply place all the ingredients in a high-speed blender and blend until smooth. Serve immediately.

NUTRITION INFO
IN TOTAL:

16.9 G PROTEIN	
54.4 G FAT	
5.4 G NET CARBS	
587 KCAL	

Instant Lemon Cheesecake Yogurt Parfaits

Baking lemon cheesecake takes hours, and worse, you have to wait until the next day to eat it. (Who has that kind of patience? Not me!) But these Lemon Cheesecake Yogurt Parfaits only take a minute or two to make. And their rich, sophisticated taste is absolutely decadent. So if you're craving something indulgent yet healthy and sating for breakfast, look no further than these quickie treats.

2 cups (460 g) thick, plain full-fat Turkish or Greek yogurt

½ cup (120 g) plain full-fat cream cheese

1 tablespoon (15 ml) freshly squeezed lemon juice

100 drops lemon stevia, or to taste

1 cup (130 g) Grain-Free Granola, page 38, or chopped nuts of choice, plus 2 tablespoons (16 g) for garnish

—
Yield: 4 servings

Place the yogurt, cream cheese, lemon juice, and lemon stevia into a small bowl. Mix well with a spoon until smooth. Adjust the taste by adding more cream cheese, lemon juice, or lemon stevia, if necessary. Mix well again.

Place ¼ cup (32 g) of the granola or chopped nuts into four serving glasses or small mason jars, and top each with one quarter of the yogurt mixture. Garnish each with ½ tablespoon (4 g) granola and serve immediately.

NUTRITION INFO

CHOPPED WALNUTS USED IN CALCULATIONS

IN TOTAL:	
42.1 G PROTEIN	
166.2 G FAT	
28.3 G NET CARBS	
1786 KCAL	
PER SERVING, IF 4 SERVINGS IN TOTAL:	
10.5 G PROTEIN	
41.5 G FAT	
7.1 G NET CARBS	
446 KCAL	

TIP:

Not a fan of cream cheese? No problem: This recipe works just as well as a lemon yogurt parfait, minus the cream cheese. Just use 2½ cups (600 ml) plain full fat yogurt and omit the cream cheese.

Grain-Free Granola

This healthy, grain-free granola is great for your gut, and you can think of this recipe as a template for endless variations: Use whichever nuts and seeds you happen to have on hand. And feel free to reduce the amount of erythritol if you don't like your granola very sweet—but don't replace it or omit it completely because it's the secret ingredient that makes this granola deliciously crunchy.

½ cup (20 g) unsweetened coconut flakes

½ cup (45 g) almond flakes

½ cup (65 g) chopped pecans

½ cup (75 g) sunflower seeds

¼ cup (25 g) erythritol crystals

1 tablespoon (15 ml) melted extra-virgin coconut oil

1 teaspoon Ceylon cinnamon

½ teaspoon vanilla powder

—
Yield: about 2 cups (205 g)

Preheat the oven to 350°F (175°C). Line a baking sheet with parchment paper.

Place all the ingredients in a large bowl. Toss well to ensure everything is well mixed and the nuts, seeds, and coconut are covered with oil and seasonings. Transfer the mixture to the lined baking sheet, and spread it out evenly with a spoon into as thin a layer as possible.

Bake for 8 to 12 minutes, or until the mixture turns golden-brown. (Be careful, though, as the nuts can quickly become too dark and burn.) Remove the granola from the oven and let cool completely. The granola is soft and chewy while hot, but becomes crunchy when it has cooled down.

Break the cool granola into small pieces, and store in a tightly sealed glass jar in a cool, dry place.

NUTRITION INFO

IN TOTAL:	
34.4 G PROTEIN	
132.9 G FAT	
17.9 G NET CARBS	
1411 KCAL	
PER ¼ CUP (25 G):	
4.3 G PROTEIN	
16.6 G FAT	
2.2 G NET CARBS	
176 KCAL	
PER TABLESPOON (6 G):	
1.1 G PROTEIN	
4.2 G FAT	
0.6 G NET CARBS	
44 KCAL	

TIP:

Make Pumpkin Pie Spiced Grain-Free Granola. It's easy: Just replace the cinnamon with pumpkin pie spice.

Starch-Free Hot Cereal

If you're following a gluten-free, low-sugar diet, a traditional breakfast of porridge or oatmeal isn't an option. But this simple, healthy alternative is just as good—and it's packed with nutrients, too. Top it with berries, sugar-free syrup, or a sizeable pat of grass-fed butter, and you've got a warming, satisfying, low-carb breakfast that'll see you through even the darkest winter mornings.

⅓ cup (80 g) unsweetened almond butter

2 teaspoons milled chia seeds

⅓ cup (80 ml) water

1 pinch unrefined sea salt or Himalayan salt, or to taste

—
Yield: 1 serving

Combine all ingredients in a small saucepan, and place over a medium-low heat, stirring continuously and breaking the almond butter lumps into smaller pieces with the back of a spoon.

When the mixture is smooth, hot, and thick, remove the saucepan from the heat. Let cool slightly, and serve with fresh berries or a pat of grass-fed butter, if you like.

TIP:

Almond butter suits this hot "cereal" especially well, but feel free to experiment with different nut butters.

NUTRITION INFO

IN TOTAL:

18.4 G PROTEIN

46.3 G FAT

5.4 G NET CARBS

511 KCAL

NOTE:

Mix things up a little: use unsweetened almond milk or heavy cream instead of water for a richer taste.

Luscious Low-Sugar French Toast

Just a quick glance at the ingredient list for classic French toast confirms that it's full of sugar and starch—a major no-no if you're following a low-sugar lifestyle. But my healthy version tastes just as good—even better!—and has practically no sugar at all. Be sure to use a sufficiently high heat for frying to keep your French toast from getting soggy.

FOR THE FRENCH TOAST:

4 eggs

¼ cup (60 ml) unsweetened almond milk

1 teaspoon vanilla extract

1 teaspoon Ceylon cinnamon

5 drops liquid stevia

8 slices Easy Fluffy Bread (page 24)

Butter for frying

FOR TOPPING:

Freshly grated nutmeg (optional)

¼ cup (60 g) grass-fed butter

⅓ cup (80 ml) Homemade Sugar-Free Maple Syrup, page 23

—
Yield: 4 servings

Prepare the French toast. Place the eggs, almond milk, vanilla extract, cinnamon, and stevia in a medium bowl. Whisk well to combine. (If the cinnamon floats on top of the mixture, just continue to whisk until it has become well incorporated.) Then soak each bread slice in the egg mixture for 10 seconds.

Heat a griddle or skillet over medium-high heat. When hot, melt a pat of butter in the skillet. Fry the bread slices for 3 to 4 minutes on each side, or until golden brown. To serve, sprinkle each slice of French toast with freshly grated nutmeg, if you like, and top with a pat of butter and Homemade Sugar-Free Maple Syrup (page 23).

TIP:

Making French toast for the holidays? Replace the almond milk with ⅓ cup (80 ml) Rich Sugar-Free Eggnog (page 137) or use Low-Sugar Cinnamon Raisin Bread (page 25) instead of Easy Fluffy Bread.

NOTE:

Sprinkle shaved dark chocolate (with a minimum cocoa content of 85 percent) on the freshly fried bread slices. The chocolate melts and creates an incredibly chocolatey—but guilt-free!—treat.

NUTRITION INFO

IN TOTAL:

79.6 G PROTEIN	
176.2 G FAT	
14.5 G NET CARBS	
1963 KCAL	

PER SERVING,
IF 4 SERVINGS IN TOTAL:

19.9 G PROTEIN	
44.0 G FAT	
3.6 G NET CARBS	
491 KCAL	

Splendid Sun-Dried Tomato, Basil, and Pine Nut Muffins

Bursting with fresh flavors, these breakfast muffins are a wonderfully savory way to start your day. They're topped with piquant pine nuts, spotted with bold basil, and dotted with succulent sun-dried tomatoes. They're baked at a low oven temperature, so they're exceptionally moist. Make them ahead of time and freeze them. In the morning, all you need to do is pop a couple into the microwave, and you're good to go.

½ cup (60 g) coconut flour

2 teaspoons aluminum-free baking powder

1 teaspoon onion powder

6 eggs

½ cup (20 g) finely chopped fresh basil leaves, loosely packed

⅓ cup (35 g) finely chopped sun-dried tomatoes

¼ cup (60 ml) heavy cream or coconut cream

½ teaspoon unrefined sea salt or Himalayan salt, or to taste

2 tablespoons (18 g) pine nuts

—
Yield: 10 muffins

Preheat the oven to 300°F (150°C). Line a muffin pan with paper liners.

Combine the coconut flour, baking powder, and onion powder in a small bowl. Mix well to break up any lumps.

Place the eggs, basil, tomatoes, cream, and salt in a medium bowl. Whisk well until combined. Gradually add the dry ingredients to the wet, whisking all the time to prevent lumping.

Scoop the batter into the muffin liners, filling them three-quarters full. Top each with a sprinkle of pine nuts, gently pressing the nuts into the muffin batter so that they stick. Bake for 20 to 30 minutes, or until a toothpick inserted in the middle of a muffin comes out almost dry. Don't overbake. Remove from the oven, let cool, and serve warm.

NUTRITION INFO

IN TOTAL:

65.1 G PROTEIN	
87.8 G FAT	
27.4 G NET CARBS	
1167 KCAL	

PER MUFFIN,
IF 10 MUFFINS IN TOTAL:

6.5 G PROTEIN	
8.8 G FAT	
2.7 G NET CARBS	
117 KCAL	

Hearty Breakfast Muffins with Bacon and Cheese

These stick-to-your-ribs breakfast muffins are a dream come true for busy mornings. Prepare them beforehand and freeze. When hunger hits, just pop one in the microwave, then grab and go. Because they're sure to tide you over till dinner, they make a great take-along midafternoon snack for school or work, too. There's no need to stick to bacon and cheese here, either. You can create endless variations using different cheeses, meats, or veggies.

¼ cup (30 g) coconut flour

1 teaspoon aluminum-free baking powder

1 teaspoon onion powder

1 teaspoon Cajun seasoning

5 eggs

¼ cup (60 ml) heavy cream

1½ cups (145 g) shredded Swiss cheese (or other sharp cheese)

1 cup (140 g) chopped raw bacon

½ teaspoon unrefined sea salt, or to taste

¼ cup (55 g) finely chopped pickled, drained jalapeños (optional)

—
Yield: 8 to 12 muffins

Preheat the oven to 350°F (175°C).
Line a muffin pan with paper liners.

Combine the coconut flour and the baking powder in a small bowl, then mix the rest of the ingredients in a large bowl until well mixed. Add the coconut flour mixture to the bowl with the rest of the ingredients and mix with a fork until the batter is smooth.

Scoop the batter into the muffin liners, filling them three-quarters full. Bake for 20 minutes, or until a toothpick inserted in the center of a muffin comes out almost dry. Remove from the oven, let cool slightly, and serve warm. Freeze the leftovers.

NOTE:

These muffins are really hearty and satisfying, so serve them with some raw veggies, such as carrots or celery sticks, for a well-balanced breakfast or snack.

NUTRITION INFO

IN TOTAL:

105.8 G PROTEIN	
138.6 G FAT	
11.4 G NET CARBS	
1717 KCAL	

PER MUFFIN, IF 8 MUFFINS IN TOTAL:	PER MUFFIN, IF 12 MUFFINS IN TOTAL:
13.2 G PROTEIN	8.8 G PROTEIN
17.3 G FAT	11.6 G FAT
1.4 G NET CARBS	1.0 G NET CARBS
215 KCAL	143 KCAL

Scrummy Streusel-Topped Blueberry Muffins

Topped with lip-licking streusel, sugar-free blueberry muffins have never tasted this good before! Here's why: This recipe uses a lower oven temperature to prevent the (starch-free) streusel from getting too dark, and to keep the muffins deliciously moist. Wild blueberries are the most nutritious—and the most natural—option, so go for them if you can find them.

FOR THE STREUSEL:

¾ cup (90 g) chopped pecans

2 tablespoons (26 g) erythritol crystals

½ teaspoon Ceylon cinnamon

1½ tablespoons (25 ml) melted grass-fed butter or extra-virgin coconut oil

FOR THE MUFFINS:

4 eggs

⅓ cup (80 ml) heavy cream or coconut milk

⅓ cup (33 g) erythritol crystals

20 drops vanilla stevia, or to taste

½ cup (60 g) coconut flour

½ cup (75 g) frozen wild blueberries

—
Yield: 10 muffins

Preheat the oven to 300°F (150°C). Line a muffin pan with paper liners.

Prepare the streusel: Combine all the streusel ingredients in a medium bowl. Mix well with a spoon. Set aside.

Prepare the muffin batter: Place the eggs, cream, erythritol, and vanilla stevia in a medium bowl and mix well. Gradually add the coconut flour, mixing all the time to prevent lumping. Fold in the frozen blueberries. Scoop the batter into the muffin liners, filling them three-quarters full. Divide the streusel between the muffins, gently pressing it into the muffin batter so it sticks. Bake for 30 to 40 minutes, or until a toothpick inserted in the middle of a muffin comes out almost dry. Remove from the oven, let cool slightly, and serve, or freeze for 1 to 2 months.

NUTRITION INFO

WITH STREUSEL	*WITHOUT STREUSEL*
IN TOTAL:	IN TOTAL:
53.7 G PROTEIN	44.5 G PROTEIN
145.8 G FAT	62.5 G FAT
24.1 G NET CARBS	19.6 G NET CARBS
1635 KCAL	827 KCAL
PER MUFFIN, IF 10 MUFFINS IN TOTAL:	PER MUFFIN, IF 10 MUFFINS IN TOTAL:
5.3 G PROTEIN	4.4 G PROTEIN
14.6 G FAT	6.3 G FAT
2.5 G NET CARBS	2.0 G NET CARBS
164 KCAL	83 KCAL

Quick Pizza Omelet

Wait a minute! Pizza for breakfast? That's right—and there's no need to feel guilty about this low-carb version. It's big on protein and healthy fats, and best of all, it's easy to change up: Just use different meats, cheeses, veggies, or whatever leftovers happen to be lurking in the fridge. This recipe makes a satisfying breakfast for one ravenous person—or two moderately hungry ones.

2 tablespoons (28 ml) heavy cream

¼ teaspoon garlic powder

¼ teaspoon onion powder

Unrefined sea salt, to taste

2 eggs

1 tablespoon (14 g) grass-fed butter or extra-virgin coconut oil, for frying

2 tablespoons (31 g) unsweetened tomato sauce

3 slices ham or pepperoni (or more or less to taste)

5 black Kalamata olives, pitted and sliced

1½ ounces (45 g) shredded mozzarella cheese

¼ teaspoon dried oregano

—
Yield: 2 servings

Mix the cream, garlic powder, onion powder, and salt together until well-combined and free from lumps. Add the eggs and mix gently with a fork.

Heat a skillet over medium heat and melt the butter or coconut oil in it. Pour the egg mixture into the skillet and cook, carefully pushing the cooked parts at the edges toward the center with a spatula. When the omelet is done around the edges but still jelly-like at the center, top with the tomato sauce, ham or pepperoni, olives, cheese, and oregano. Cover and cook for 2 minutes more, or until the cheese is melted. Serve immediately.

NUTRITION INFO

IN TOTAL:

32.7 G PROTEIN	
36.2 G FAT	
5.5 G NET CARBS	
480 KCAL	

PER SERVING,
IF 2 SERVINGS IN TOTAL:

16.3 G PROTEIN	
18.1 G FAT	
2.8 G NET CARBS	
240 KCAL	

Puffy Cheese Omelet with Avocado

The secret to an impressively puffy omelet is to bake it in the oven with a bowl filled with boiling water, to mimic a water bath. The result? A simple, filling breakfast that's perfect for weekends: Just pop the omelet into the oven, then chill out over coffee and the newspaper for half an hour or so until breakfast is ready.

Softened butter (for greasing the dish)

6 eggs

2 cups (155 g) shredded cheddar cheese or other sharp cheese

⅔ cup (160 ml) heavy cream

½ cup (120 ml) unsweetened almond milk

1 teaspoon unrefined sea salt or Himalayan salt, or to taste

2 ripe Hass avocados, peeled, pitted and sliced

—
Yield: 6 servings

Preheat the oven to 350°F (175°C). Grease a 1.5-quart (1.5 L) baking dish generously with softened butter.

Place the eggs, cheese, heavy cream, almond milk, and salt in a large bowl. Whisk until well mixed, then pour the mixture into the greased baking dish. Sprinkle the cheese evenly on top.

Place a small, shallow, ovenproof bowl on the lowest oven rack. Carefully fill the bowl three-quarters full with boiling water. Place the baking dish with the omelet mixture on the middle oven rack.

Bake for 30 to 40 minutes, or until the center is no longer wobbly. (Don't overbake, though, as the eggs will turn out too dry. If the surface starts to become too brown, cover the dish with aluminum foil.) Remove from the oven and let cool slightly. Serve warm, topped with avocado slices.

NUTRITION INFO

IN TOTAL:	
93.6 G PROTEIN	
180.7 G FAT	
7.4 G NET CARBS	
2049 KCAL	
PER SERVING, IF 6 SERVINGS IN TOTAL:	
15.6 G PROTEIN	
30.1 G FAT	
1.2 G NET CARBS	
341 KCAL	

TIP:

You can add more fillings to the omelet, such as ham, sausage, cooked veggies, or bits and pieces of leftover cheese.

Five-Ingredient Overnight Sausage and Egg Breakfast Casserole

Ripe tomatoes give this meaty, five-ingredient casserole a summery lift. Just be sure to choose firm ones: If your tomatoes are too ripe and soft, they might release too much liquid during baking. Patience is a virtue here, by the way. After removing the casserole from the oven, it's important to let it stand for 15 minutes before serving to keep the moisture from leaking out. It'll be worth the wait—I promise.

1 pound (450 g) spicy bulk sausage

2 small firm Roma tomatoes, diced

2 cups (250 g) shredded mozzarella cheese

6 eggs

½ cup (120 ml) heavy cream

Unrefined sea salt or Himalayan salt and freshly ground black pepper, to taste

—

Yield: 6 servings

Fry the sausage until cooked through, crumbling it with a wooden fork while frying. Spread the cooked sausage evenly into a 2-quart (2 L) baking dish. Top with the diced tomatoes and sprinkle the cheese on top. Mix together the eggs, heavy cream, salt, and pepper in a medium bowl. Pour the mixture evenly over the casserole. Cover, and refrigerate overnight.

When you're ready to bake the casserole, preheat the oven to 350°F (175°C). When hot, bake the casserole for 30 to 40 minutes, or until the cheese is golden brown and bubbly. Remove from the oven, let stand for 15 minutes, and then serve.

VARIATION: For an even more satisfying variation, spread 2 cups (180 g) cubed starch-free bread evenly in the bottom of the baking dish before adding the other ingredients.

NUTRITION INFO

VALUES HIGHLY DEPEND ON THE USED INGREDIENTS

IN TOTAL:

178.4 G PROTEIN

228.8 G FAT

18.3 G NET CARBS

2836 KCAL

PER SERVING,
IF 6 SERVINGS IN TOTAL:

29.7 G PROTEIN

38.1 G FAT

3.1 G NET CARBS

473 KCAL

Easy Breakfast Burrito

With some Single-Serve Tortillas (page 31) on hand, it's a snap to whip up this spicy, savory breakfast burrito—even on the busiest mornings. You can vary this burrito endlessly, too: Just use your favorite starch-free vegetables, meat or fish, and season with your choice of spices and seasonings. And it's a great way to use up the leftovers lingering in your fridge.

¼ cup (20 g) chopped button mushrooms

¼ cup (40 g) chopped green bell pepper

2 eggs

2 tablespoons (28 ml) water

1 teaspoon unsweetened sambal oelek or chili paste, or to taste

½ teaspoon onion powder

¼ teaspoon unrefined sea salt or Himalayan salt, or to taste

Oil or butter for frying

1 Single-Serve Tortilla (page 31)

2 tablespoons (30 ml) Low-Sugar Sweet and Sour Sauce (page 9)

2 tablespoons (16 g) sliced black Kalamata olives

—
Yield: 1 serving

Place the mushrooms, bell pepper, eggs, water, sambal oelek, onion powder, and salt in a medium bowl. Stir well with a fork.

Heat a skillet over medium-low heat. Add the oil or butter. When hot, add the egg mixture and cook, stirring slowly all the time, until the eggs are scrambled but still creamy. (Don't overcook or the eggs will become dry.)

Place the Single-Serve Tortilla shell on a plate and spread with the Low-Sugar Sweet and Sour Sauce on one side. Add the scrambled eggs and then top with the sliced olives. Fold the other half of the tortilla over the filling and serve immediately.

NUTRITION INFO

IN TOTAL:

25.8 G PROTEIN	
33.7 G FAT	
4.8 G NET CARBS	
425 KCAL	

Quick Chorizo and Cauliflower Breakfast Hash

There's no room for starchy potatoes in a low-sugar breakfast, but it's easy to replace them with tasty, healthy cauliflower, as in this full-bodied hash. You'll want to keep the cauliflower crunchy for the best texture and flavor here, so be sure you don't overcook it. Serve this simple but scrumptious dish with salsa or tomato relish, if you like, and add more nonstarchy vegetables for extra nutrients.

Oil or butter for frying

1 large onion, chopped

2 garlic cloves, finely chopped

2 packages (10 ounces, or 280 g, each) frozen cauliflower florets

10 ounces (280 g) chorizo, chopped

4 eggs

Unrefined sea salt or Himalayan salt and freshly ground black pepper, to taste

—

Yield: 2 to 4 servings

Heat a skillet over medium-high heat. Add the oil or butter. When hot, add the onion and garlic. Cook until soft and translucent, about 5 minutes. Add the cauliflower and cook, mixing, until the cauliflower is hot. Don't overcook. Add the chorizo and cook, stirring, until the chorizo is slightly browned. Season with salt and pepper.

Fry the eggs in a separate skillet but keep the chorizo and cauliflower hash warm while doing so. Transfer the hash to serving plates and top each serving with a fried egg. Serve immediately.

NUTRITION INFO

IN TOTAL:

108.4 G PROTEIN

122.2 G FAT

29.1 G NET CARBS

1639 KCAL

PER SERVING,
IF 2 SERVINGS IN TOTAL:

54.2 G PROTEIN

61.1 G FAT

14.5 G NET CARBS

820 KCAL

PER SERVING,
IF 4 SERVINGS IN TOTAL:

27.1 G PROTEIN

30.6 G FAT

7.3 G NET CARBS

410 KCAL

Fifteen-Minute Spring Vegetable and Feta Breakfast Hash

Artichokes are to spring what butterflies are to summer, but preparing them from scratch is too much work for a busy morning. That's where canned artichoke hearts come in, offering all their characteristic sweetness and flavor. They shine alongside asparagus and radishes in this healthy vegetarian hash, which gets crowned with sliced avocado and tangy feta cheese.

1 tablespoon (15 ml) extra-virgin olive oil

1 small zucchini (7 ounces, or 200 g), cubed

1 teaspoon onion powder

½ teaspoon garlic powder

14-ounce (400 g) can artichoke hearts, drained (large ones quartered; medium and small ones halved)

8 green asparagus spears, woody stems removed, and cut into 2-inch (5 cm) pieces

10 radishes, halved

½ teaspoon unrefined sea salt or Himalayan salt

4 ounces (115 g) feta cheese, crumbled

2 Hass avocados, peeled, pitted, and sliced

1 tablespoon (15 ml) freshly squeezed lemon juice

1 cup (20 g) chopped watercress

—
Yield: 2 servings

Add the oil to a skillet and place over medium-high heat. Add the zucchini, onion powder, and garlic powder. Cook, covered, until the zucchini is crisp-tender, about 5 minutes. Add the artichoke, asparagus, and radishes. Heat, stirring, until hot, but don't cook. Season with salt, and divide the hash between two serving plates. Sprinkle each with half the feta.

Arrange the sliced avocado on top of both servings, one avocado per serving. Drizzle the lemon juice on the avocado slices to prevent them from turning brown. Top both servings with watercress and serve immediately.

NUTRITION INFO

IN TOTAL:

42.6 G PROTEIN	
87.1 G FAT	
17.7 G NET CARBS	
1025 KCAL	

PER SERVING, IF 2 SERVINGS IN TOTAL:

21.3 G PROTEIN	
43.5 G FAT	
8.8 G NET CARBS	
512 KCAL	

NOTE:

Need more protein? Serve the breakfast hash with fried eggs.

CHAPTER 3

Lunch

Whether you spend your day in the office or at home, having a satisfying lunch is a must in order to keep your energy levels up for the rest of the day. And if you're following a low-sugar lifestyle, you don't want to rely on your local burger joint or the sandwich bar down the street. Luckily, this chapter features plenty of low-sugar lunch recipes that are super portable as well as quick and easy to prepare, such as soups, salads, sandwiches, and wraps.

Comforting Chicken Zoodle Soup

Nourishing, homemade chicken noodle soup is the ultimate cure for just about any ailment. So, when lunchtime rolls around, grab a mug of this healthy, gluten-free, starch-free chicken zoodle soup, wrap yourself in a cozy blanket (unless you're at the office!), and let the healing begin.

2 tablespoons (28 g) extra-virgin coconut oil

1 small onion, chopped

2 garlic cloves, minced

2 celery stalks, thinly sliced

½ teaspoon dried thyme

1 bay leaf

1½ quarts (1.4 L) chicken stock

6 black peppercorns

1½ ounces (45 g) carrot, cut into matchsticks

2 cups (440 g) shredded cooked chicken

Unrefined sea salt or Himalayan salt, to taste

7 ounces (200 g) zoodles (spiralized zucchini)

Finely chopped fresh parsley for garnish (optional)

—
Yield: 8 servings

Heat a large saucepan over medium heat and add the coconut oil, followed by the onion, garlic, celery, thyme, and bay leaf. Cook, stirring, for 5 minutes or until the onion is translucent. (Don't let it brown.) Add the chicken stock, peppercorns, and carrots and bring to a boil. Let simmer for 5 minutes.

Add the chicken and simmer until the chicken is heated through. Season with salt, add the zoodles, and stir well. (Don't continue to cook: The zoodles will easily turn mushy if cooked.) Serve immediately. Garnish each serving with fresh parsley, if you wish.

TIP:

If you don't have cooked chicken on hand, you can cook 22 ounces (625 g) of raw, diced chicken in a skillet until the juices run clear and then use it in this light soup.

NUTRITION INFO

IN TOTAL:	
136.4 G PROTEIN	
64.6 G FAT	
6.7 G NET CARBS	
1153 KCAL	
PER SERVING, IF 8 SERVINGS IN TOTAL:	
17.0 G PROTEIN	
8.1 G FAT	
0.8 G NET CARBS	
144 KCAL	

Easy Bouillabaisse

Bouillabaisse is a traditional French soup that features fish, seafood, and vegetables, as well as Provençal herbs. The fish used in classic bouillabaisse is usually bony, but feel free to use any type of fish you like—or even a number of different types, which adds dimension and variation. You can also replace the mussels with other seafood, or use canned mussels or clams if you can't find fresh ones.

¼ cup (60 ml) extra-virgin olive oil

1 large onion, chopped

2 garlic cloves, crushed

14-ounce (400 g) can crushed or diced tomatoes

1 small fennel bulb, cut into strips

6 cups (1.4 L) fish stock

8 saffron threads

1 teaspoon dried thyme

1 tablespoon (6 g) freshly grated orange peel (orange part only), optional

1½ pounds (680 g) fish of your choice, cut into bite-size pieces

1 pound (450 g) shell-on mussels, scrubbed and debearded (dead mussels discarded)

2 teaspoons unrefined sea salt or Himalayan salt, or to taste

½ cup (30 g) chopped flat leaf parsley, loosely packed

—
Yield: 6 to 8 servings

Heat a large saucepan over medium-high heat. Add the olive oil, onion, and garlic. Cook, stirring, until translucent, about 5 minutes.

Add the tomatoes and bring to a boil. Then add the fennel, fish stock, saffron, thyme, and orange peel, if using. Lower the heat and simmer until the fennel is crisp-tender, about 10 to 15 minutes.

Add the fish and the mussels. Simmer, covered, until the fish flakes, and the mussels open, about 5 to 10 minutes. Discard any unopened mussels. Season with salt and garnish with parsley.

NOTE:

To serve the soup in the traditional way, serve the bouillon first alongside starch-free bread, such as Easy Fluffy Bread (page 24). Serve the fish on a separate plate after the bouillon.

NUTRITION INFO

HALIBUT USED IN CALCULATIONS FOR FISH	PER SERVING, IF 6 SERVINGS IN TOTAL:	PER SERVING, IF 8 SERVINGS IN TOTAL:
IN TOTAL:	26.0 G PROTEIN	19.5 G PROTEIN
156.2 G PROTEIN	11.7 G FAT	8.8 G FAT
70.1 G FAT	6.3 G NET CARBS	4.8 G NET CARBS
38.1 G NET CARBS	241 KCAL	180 KCAL
1443 KCAL		

Fifteen-Minute Thai-Inspired Pumpkin Soup

Spicy, warming, and hearty, this five-ingredient soup is ready in no time. Prepare it in the morning and store a serving in an insulated food jar until lunchtime (the flavors improve when they have time to mingle for a couple of hours). For a little variation, try experimenting with different types of curry paste: Red, green, and yellow curry pastes all work well here. Top with a dollop of sour cream and a small handful of crumbled bacon for extra flavor and satiety.

2 cans (15 ounces, or 425 g, each) 100 percent pure pumpkin puree

1 to 2 tablespoons (15 to 30 g) Thai red curry paste

1 teaspoon onion powder

1 teaspoon unrefined sea salt or Himalayan salt, or to taste

1 cup (240 ml) heavy cream

Water, if necessary

—
Yield: 4 servings

Combine the pumpkin, curry paste, onion powder, salt, and heavy cream in a large saucepan. Mix until smooth. If necessary, add a little water for a thinner consistency. Heat over medium-high heat, stirring constantly. When the mixture starts to boil, reduce the heat to a minimum. Let it simmer for 5 to 10 minutes, until thoroughly hot. Serve with gluten-free low-sugar bread or crackers.

NUTRITION INFO

IN TOTAL:

22.0 G PROTEIN	
87.4 G FAT	
33.9 G NET CARBS	
1014 KCAL	

PER SERVING, IF 4 SERVINGS IN TOTAL:

5.5 G PROTEIN	
21.9 G FAT	
8.5 G NET CARBS	
253 KCAL	

Rich No-Potato Clam Chowder

There's no need to use starchy potatoes to make the perfect clam chowder. Here, super-healthy cauliflower replaces tasteless, carb-laden potatoes, and there are no starchy thickeners, either; pureed cauliflower does the trick instead, while heavy cream adds richness and extra body. If you don't have clam juice, don't skip it or replace it with water. Use fish stock or bouillon instead.

6 cups (670 g) cauliflower chopped into ½-inch (1.3 cm) chunks, divided

8 slices raw bacon

1 cup (170 g) diced carrots

¾ cup (100 g) finely chopped onion

¾ cup (120 g) diced celery

2 cans (6.5 ounces, or 184 g, each) minced clams

6.5-ounce (184 g) can chopped clams

2 cups (480 ml) heavy cream

2 cups (480 ml) clam juice

1 teaspoon unrefined sea salt or Himalayan salt, or to taste

Freshly ground white pepper

1 tablespoon (15 ml) fresh lemon juice (optional)

—

Yield: 8 servings

Cook 3 cups (335 g) of the chopped cauliflower until soft and tender. Carefully discard the water. In a blender, process the cauliflower into a smooth puree. Set aside.

Fry the bacon until crisp. Reserve the fat and set the bacon aside. Fry the carrots, onion, celery, and the remaining cauliflower in the bacon fat until slightly soft, about 5 minutes.

Meanwhile, drain the juice from the clams into a large saucepan. Add the heavy cream and the pureed cauliflower. Mix well and bring to a boil.

Add the cooked vegetables with the bacon fat to the saucepan and cook until tender, about 10 to 15 minutes. Add the clams and remove from the heat. (Don't cook the clams: they'll become tough.) Season with salt and pepper. Add 1 tablespoon (15 ml) fresh lemon juice if you prefer a slightly tangy flavor. Serve immediately, crumbling some of the bacon on top of each serving.

NUTRITION INFO

IN TOTAL:

129.5 G PROTEIN	
218.7 G FAT	
60.4 G NET CARBS	
2764 KCAL	

PER SERVING, IF 8 SERVINGS IN TOTAL:

16.2 G PROTEIN	
27.3 G FAT	
7.6 G NET CARBS	
345 KCAL	

TIP:

When choosing canned clams, be sure to select a version that's additive-free. Most canned clams contain sodium tripolyphosphate, which helps retain the clams' natural juices, and calcium disodium EDTA, to maintain color. So try to find a product that consists only of clams, salt, and water, but if you can't, choose whole clams and chop half of them into tiny pieces and half of them into larger chunks.

Pasta-Free Minestrone with Ham

Minestrone is back! This "healthified" version of the classic Italian soup won't spike your blood sugar levels, and it won't stress out your gut. Instead, it'll pamper it with plenty of fiber and healthy fats. This soup isn't technically pasta-free, since it includes low-carb shirataki noodles, but it *is* free from the starchy noodles essential to the traditional version.

2 tablespoons (28 ml) extra-virgin olive oil

1 large onion, chopped

2 garlic cloves, crushed

1 cup (105 g) sliced celery stalks

½ cup (80 g) diced carrot

4 cups (950 ml) chicken or vegetable stock

14-ounce (400 g) can crushed
or diced tomatoes

1 cup (120 g) frozen green beans

2 packages (7 ounces, or 200 g, each)
shirataki fettucine or tagliatelle, cooked and
cut into 2-inch (5 cm) pieces

1½ cups (205 g) chopped ham

1 teaspoon unrefined sea salt
or Himalayan salt, or to taste

¼ cup (10 g) chopped fresh basil leaves

Freshly grated Parmesan cheese, for serving
(optional)

—
Yield: 6 servings

Heat a large saucepan over medium heat. Add the olive oil, onion, garlic, celery, and carrot. Cook until the onion is translucent, about 5 minutes. Add the stock and the crushed tomatoes and bring to a boil. Then add the green beans, shirataki, and ham. Reduce the heat to medium-low. Let simmer, covered, until the vegetables are tender, about 20 minutes. Season with salt. Serve with a sprinkling of chopped fresh basil and some grated Parmesan, if desired.

NUTRITION INFO

WITHOUT PARMESAN

IN TOTAL:

| 45.9 G PROTEIN |
| 37.4 G FAT |
| 32.9 G NET CARBS |
| 650 KCAL |

PER SERVING,
IF 6 SERVINGS IN TOTAL:

| 7.7 G PROTEIN |
| 6.2 G FAT |
| 5.5 G NET CARBS |
| 108 KCAL |

Effortless Egg Salad Sandwich

Great for kids and grownups alike, this easy-to-make egg salad is a lunchtime crowd-pleaser. Make it a day or two in advance so that you'll have it on hand for an instant lunchbox filler. Then use it to make sandwiches with slices of Easy Fluffy Bread (page 24), wrap, and you're good to go. Add some raw veggies for a well-rounded meal. Carrot and celery sticks provide a nice crunch.

FOR EGG SALAD:

8 eggs

½ cup (113 g) Foolproof One-Minute Mayo (page 12)

1 teaspoon dry mustard (that is, mustard powder or ground mustard seeds)

3 tablespoons (9 g) chopped chives

½ teaspoon unrefined sea salt or Himalayan salt, or to taste

OTHER INGREDIENTS:

8 slices Easy Fluffy Bread (page 24)

—
Yield: 4 servings

First, prepare the egg salad. Place the eggs in a large saucepan and cover with cold water. Cover with a lid. Bring the water to a boil, but remove the saucepan from the heat immediately when boiling starts. Let the eggs stand covered in hot water for 10 to 12 minutes.

Remove the eggs from the hot water and let cool completely in cold water. When the eggs are cool, peel them, place them on a large, shallow plate, and mash with a fork. Add the mayonnaise, mustard, and chives and stir until well mixed. Season with salt.

Divide the egg salad among 4 slices of bread. Spread the mixture evenly. Top each with one of the remaining bread slices to make sandwiches. Wrap the sandwiches in wax paper or plastic wrap and keep refrigerated until serving time.

NUTRITION INFO

IN TOTAL:	
106.2 G PROTEIN	
184.9 G FAT	
13.4 G NET CARBS	
2143 KCAL	
PER SANDWICH, IF 4 SANDWICHES IN TOTAL:	
26.6 G PROTEIN	
46.2 G FAT	
3.3 G NET CARBS	
536 KCAL	

TIP:

To make curried egg salad, just replace the chives with 1 teaspoon of curry powder.

Five-Ingredient Avocado, Bleu Cheese, and Pecan Salad

Ridiculously low in sugar but packed with full-on flavors, this simple salad is rich in healthy fats, thanks to the avocado and pecans. And both are a great match for rich, creamy bleu cheese, which adds a dose of decadence to the mix. Dress this salad with Quick Raspberry Vinaigrette (page 14) and serve it as a light lunch, or add cooked, cubed chicken or shrimp for a more satiating meal.

2 cups (65 g) mixed salad greens, loosely packed

2 cups (60 g) fresh spinach leaves, loosely packed

1 medium Hass avocado, peeled, pitted, and cubed

¼ cup (60 g) crumbled unpasteurized bleu cheese

⅓ cup (60 g) chopped toasted pecans

—
Yield: 2 servings

Arrange all the ingredients on a serving plate (or in a mason jar, for a portable version). Store in the fridge until ready to serve. Serve with Quick Raspberry Vinaigrette (page 14), or your favorite tangy salad dressing.

NUTRITION INFO

IN TOTAL:

22.7 G PROTEIN	
79.4 G FAT	
4.1 G NET CARBS	
832 KCAL	

PER SERVING,
IF 2 SERVINGS IN TOTAL:

11.3 G PROTEIN	
39.7 G FAT	
2.1 G NET CARBS	
416 KCAL	

Greek Salad with Chicken and Strawberries

The perfect lunch for a sunny summer's day, this classic Greek salad gets freshened up with a scattering of juicy strawberries. But it's still plenty filling, thanks to the cooked chicken and tangy feta cheese. If you're taking it with you for lunch—on a picnic, perhaps?—be sure to store the salad and the dressing in separate containers to keep the salad from wilting.

FOR THE SALAD:

1 head iceberg lettuce, cut into thin strips

1 small red onion, thinly sliced

½ English cucumber, thinly sliced

4 small tomatoes, cut into wedges

16 black Kalamata olives

4 ounces (115 g) feta cheese, cubed

4 ounces (115 g) cooked chicken, cubed

7 ounces (200 g) fresh strawberries, cut into wedges

OTHER INGREDIENTS:

¼ cup (60 ml) Fantastic French Dressing (page 13), to serve

—
Yield: 4 servings

Arrange the ingredients on four serving plates in the given order. Serve immediately with Fantastic French Dressing.

TIP:

Make this a classic Greek salad by omitting the chicken, increasing the amount of feta to 7 ounces (200 g), and omitting the strawberries (although the strawberries do add a fresh, summery, succulent taste).

NUTRITION INFO

WITH FANTASTIC FRENCH DRESSING	WITHOUT FANTASTIC FRENCH DRESSING
IN TOTAL:	IN TOTAL:
61.2 G PROTEIN	60.9 G PROTEIN
104.9 G FAT	56.5 G FAT
35.3 G NET CARBS	34.8 G NET CARBS
1340 KCAL	901 KCAL
PER SERVING, IF 4 SERVINGS IN TOTAL:	PER SERVING, IF 4 SERVINGS IN TOTAL:
15.3 G PROTEIN	15.2 G PROTEIN
26.2 G FAT	14.1 G FAT
8.8 G NET CARBS	8.7 G NET CARBS
335 KCAL	225 KCAL

NOTE:

Feeling fruity? For a merrier, berrier version of this salad, serve it with the Quick Raspberry Vinaigrette on page 14.

Bold Beef Salad

Red meat often gets a bad rap. But the truth is that unprocessed red meat contains an ample amount of vitamins and nutrients, and can be part of a healthy diet when consumed in moderation. Try to buy grass-fed beef, if you can: It's more natural, and therefore healthier. And it's delicious in this salad, which, true to its name, is full of bold colors and flavors.

1 tablespoon (15 ml) extra-virgin olive oil

4 ounces (115 g) beef sirloin,
cut into bite-size strips

½ teaspoon unrefined sea salt
or Himalayan salt, or to taste

Pinch freshly ground black pepper

½ red bell pepper, chopped

½ teaspoon onion powder

3 cups (100 g) mixed salad greens

1 cup (50 g) chopped Belgian endive

¼ cup (20 g) tightly packed
arugula leaves (optional)

¼ cup (30 g) chopped pecans

—
Yield: 1 serving

Prepare the beef for the salad. Heat a skillet over high heat. Add the olive oil and the beef and cook until medium-well done. Season with salt and pepper. Remove the meat from the skillet and set aside.

Reduce the heat to medium. Add the bell pepper and the onion powder. Mix well and cook until the bell pepper is crisp-tender. Season with salt and pepper. Combine the beef and the bell pepper mixture and set aside to cool. (Reserve the grease from the pan and use it for other purposes, or add it to the salad dressing for extra flavor and healthy fats.)

Prepare the salad. Arrange the salad greens and the endive (and the arugula, if using) on a serving plate. Top with the beef and bell pepper mixture.
Top the salad with the pecans. Serve immediately with a low-sugar dressing, such as Fantastic French Dressing (page 13) or Quick Raspberry Vinaigrette (page 14).

NUTRITION INFO

IN TOTAL:

27.6 G PROTEIN

43.3 G FAT

4.3 G NET CARBS

522 KCAL

Quick Tuna Satay Sandwich

In Thailand, a typical satay meal consists of bread, meat, satay sauce, and cucumber onion relish. And these sandwiches contain all of the above—except they're made with starch-free Easy Fluffy Bread (page 24), so they're far healthier, but just as tasty. Oh, and a word of caution: Be sure to drain the tuna well, since the salad might separate if any water is left.

FOR TUNA SATAY SALAD:

6.5-ounce (185 g) can albacore tuna in water, drained

½ cup (120 ml) Simple and Succulent Satay Sauce (page 16)

2 teaspoons raw apple cider vinegar

Pinch cayenne pepper

¼ cup chopped fresh cilantro (optional)

OTHER INGREDIENTS:

8 slices Easy Fluffy Bread (page 24)

2-inch (5 cm) piece English cucumber, thinly sliced

1 small onion, thinly sliced

Yield: 4 servings

First, prepare the tuna satay salad. Place all the ingredients in a small bowl. Mix well and set aside.

Prepare the sandwiches. Place four slices of Easy Fluffy Bread on a plate. Divide the cucumber slices, then the onion slices evenly between the bread slices. Top each with equal portions of the tuna satay salad, then top each with the remaining slices of bread. Wrap the sandwiches in wax paper or plastic wrap and keep refrigerated until serving time.

TIP:

To make chicken satay sandwiches, just replace the tuna with shredded chicken.

NUTRITION INFO

IN TOTAL:

100.5 G PROTEIN

95.2 G FAT

25.9 G NET CARBS

1363 KCAL

PER SANDWICH,
IF 4 SANDWICHES IN TOTAL:

25.1 G PROTEIN

23.8 G FAT

6.5 G NET CARBS

341 KCAL

Irresistible Curried Vegetable Wrap

Could this be the most delicious veggie wrap in the world? Possibly. It's filled with low-starch vegetables cooked quickly in a creamy coconut sauce, plus alfalfa sprouts for extra crunch, bulk, and nutrition. Feel free to prepare the vegetable sauce alone and serve it alongside a handful of starch-free crackers for a warm, spoonable lunch or dinner.

½ cup (120 ml) coconut milk

2 teaspoons Thai green curry paste, or to taste

½ teaspoon onion powder

½ cup (60 g) grated zucchini

¼ cup (25 g) chopped leek

¼ cup (25 g) grated carrot

Unrefined sea salt or Himalayan salt, or to taste

4 Single-Serve Tortillas (page 31)

1 cup (20 g) alfalfa sprouts

—
Yield: 4 servings

Heat a skillet over high heat. Add the coconut milk, curry paste, and onion powder. Cook, stirring, for 1 minute until hot and smooth. Add the zucchini, leek, and carrot and cook, stirring often until the vegetables are crisp-tender and the coconut milk is reduced to a thick sauce. Season with salt.

Divide the vegetable mixture between the tortillas, spreading it into a thin, even layer. Repeat with the alfalfa sprouts. Roll into wraps, slice each in half, and serve.

NUTRITION INFO

IN TOTAL:

39.8 G PROTEIN	
49.2 G FAT	
12.1 G NET CARBS	
650 KCAL	

PER SERVING,
IF 4 SERVINGS IN TOTAL:

9.9 G PROTEIN	
12.3 G FAT	
3.0 G NET CARBS	
163 KCAL	

Terrific Teriyaki Pork Sandwich

This Asian-inflected teriyaki pork salad sandwich is bursting with flavors and textures, thanks to a hit of fresh ginger, homemade teriyaki sauce, and crunchy sesame seeds. Then it's mellowed out with a dollop of mayonnaise, and the result is nothing short of delicious. And it's a great way to use up last night's leftover cooked pork, too.

FOR TERIYAKI PORK SALAD:

½ cup (115 g) shredded cooked pork (preferably neck) or pulled pork

⅓ cup (80 g) Foolproof One-Minute Mayo (page 12)

3 tablespoons (18 g) finely chopped green onion

2 tablespoons (28 ml) No-Sugar Teriyaki Sauce (page 11)

1 tablespoon (8 g) whole sesame seeds

1 teaspoon freshly grated ginger

OTHER INGREDIENTS:

8 slices Easy Fluffy Bread (page 24)

4 lettuce leaves

—
Yield: 4 servings

First, prepare the teriyaki pork salad. Place all the ingredients in a small bowl. Mix well and set aside.

Prepare the sandwiches. Place four slices of Easy Fluffy Bread on a plate and divide the lettuce leaves between the bread slices. Top with a generous layer of teriyaki pork salad and spread evenly. Top each with the remaining slices of bread. Wrap the sandwiches in wax paper or plastic wrap and keep refrigerated until serving time.

VARIATION: Use the leftover teriyaki pork salad for making lettuce wraps: Spread the salad onto lettuce leaves, and then roll up into wraps for an easy, starch-free variation.

NUTRITION INFO

IN TOTAL:

75.7 G PROTEIN

143.6 G FAT

15.1 G NET CARBS

1664 KCAL

PER SANDWICH,
IF 4 SANDWICHES IN TOTAL:

18.9 G PROTEIN

35.9 G FAT

3.8 G NET CARBS

416 KCAL

Stellar Spinach and Cream Cheese Wrap

This super-nutritious vegetarian lunch is a great way to sneak extra green veggies into your diet. These wraps are amazingly fresh and crispy, thanks to the spinach and sesame seeds, and a good *schmear* of full-fat cream cheese means they're sating, too. And they're a great canvas for your favorite seasonings, so go ahead and dress them up with, say, chili powder, Cajun seasoning, or curry powder before rolling them up and digging in.

4 Single-Serve Tortillas (page 31)

4 ounces (115 g) full-fat cream cheese

4 teaspoons (11 g) whole sesame seeds

Unrefined sea salt or Himalayan salt and freshly ground black pepper, to taste

2 cups (60 g) fresh spinach leaves

—
Yield: 4 servings

Place each Single-Serve Tortilla on a plate and spread with 1 ounce (30 g) cream cheese. Top each with 1 teaspoon sesame seeds and season with salt and pepper. Then spread ½ cup (15 g) of the spinach leaves on each tortilla, roll them up into wraps, slice each in half, and serve.

VARIATION: For heartier wraps, add 2 ounces (60 g) lox. Divide it among the tortillas just before rolling them up into wraps.

NUTRITION INFO

IN TOTAL:

46.0 G PROTEIN

65.1 G FAT

8.0 G NET CARBS

803 KCAL

PER SERVING,
IF 4 SERVINGS IN TOTAL:

11.5 G PROTEIN

16.3 G FAT

2.0 G NET CARBS

201 KCAL

Cozy Cheeseburger Wrap

Who doesn't love a juicy cheeseburger? The traditional versions, unfortunately, are far from healthy, not least because of their starchy buns. But these low-carb cheeseburger wraps—which include all the trimmings—are comfort food at its best. Treat yourself to them for a special at-home lunch, or whip up a whole batch for dinner, and let family members make their own wraps at the table.

6 ounces (170 g) ground beef

Oil or butter for frying

½ teaspoon onion powder

¼ teaspoon garlic powder

Unrefined sea salt or Himalayan salt and freshly ground black pepper, to taste

4 Single-Serve Tortillas (page 31)

¼ cup (56 g) Foolproof One-Minute Mayo (page 12)

¼ cup (50 g) finely diced tomatoes

1 cup (135 g) grated cheddar cheese

—
Yield: 4 servings

Fry the ground beef in oil or butter until cooked through and crumbly. Season with the onion powder, garlic powder, salt, and pepper. Spread each tortilla with 1 tablespoon (14 g) of mayonnaise, then top each with a quarter of the meat, tomatoes, and cheese. Roll each tortilla carefully into a wrap, slice in half, and serve immediately.

NUTRITION INFO

IN TOTAL:

102.1 G PROTEIN	
133.7 G FAT	
5.0 G NET CARBS	
1632 KCAL	

PER SERVING,
IF 4 SERVINGS IN TOTAL:

25.5 G PROTEIN	
33.4 G FAT	
1.2 G NET CARBS	
408 KCAL	

Nutritious Brie, Orange, and Walnut Wrap

To whip up this sweet-and-savory (yet low-sugar!) vegetarian wrap, all you need are a few pantry basics—such as the Low-Sugar Orange Marmalade on page 19, and a Single-Serve Tortilla. After that, it's a cinch. It makes a filling after-work or after-school snack, too—and that's a lifesaver when you're just too hungry to hang on until dinner. Or, turn it into a complete meal by adding raw vegetables or a fresh green salad on the side.

3 tablespoons (45 g) Low-Sugar Orange Marmalade (page 19)

1 Single-Serve Tortilla (page 31)

2 ounces (60 g) Brie cheese, sliced

2 tablespoons (15 g) chopped walnuts

—
Yield: 1 serving

Spread the Low-Sugar Orange Marmalade evenly over the tortilla. Top with the Brie and sprinkle the chopped walnuts on top. Roll into a tight wrap, then slice in half and serve, or wrap in parchment paper and pack for lunch.

NUTRITION INFO

IN TOTAL:
21.9 G PROTEIN
31.5 G FAT
3.8 G NET CARBS
389 KCAL

TIP:

Try other soft-ripened white cheeses, such as Camembert, in place of the Brie.

Chapter 4

Dinner

If you're coming home from work tired and hungry, spending hours in the kitchen isn't going to be on the agenda. You need a family-friendly meal that's quick, healthy, and satisfying. And the low-sugar recipes in this chapter have you covered; whether you're cooking for one person or the whole gang, you'll find plenty of options in the pages that follow.

Savory Ricotta Butternut Squash Tart

This vegetarian, egg-free pie is a perfect example of how to use starch-free thickeners as egg replacements. Here a single teaspoon of psyllium binds the filling together, resulting in a smooth, creamy texture. It took me close to ten trials to get it right, but my family and I are finally satisfied with this version. Whenever I make it, we literally can't stop eating it. If you want to reduce carbs further, or want a simpler version, omit the crust.

2 cups (250 g) grated butternut squash flesh

⅔ cup (160 g) ricotta cheese

¼ cup (60 ml) heavy cream

1 teaspoon psyllium husk powder

1 teaspoon onion powder

1 teaspoon dried thyme

1 teaspoon unrefined sea salt or Himalayan salt, or to taste

¼ teaspoon freshly grated nutmeg (optional)

1 Sugar-Free, Starch-Free Pie Crust (page 28)

—
Yield: 8 servings

Preheat the oven to 350°F (175 °C). Place the grated squash, ricotta, heavy cream, psyllium, onion powder, thyme, salt, and nutmeg, if using, into a medium bowl. Mix well and set aside.

Prepare the pie crust and prebake it (see page 28). After prebaking, pour in the filling and level the surface with a rubber spatula. Bake for 30 minutes, or until golden brown and completely set. Remove from the oven, let cool slightly, and serve warm.

NUTRITION INFO

WITH CRUST

IN TOTAL:

67.1 G PROTEIN	
215.9 G FAT	
52.0 G NET CARBS	
2420 KCAL	

PER SLICE, IF 8 SLICES IN TOTAL:

8.4 G PROTEIN	
27.0 G FAT	
6.5 G NET CARBS	
302 KCAL	

NOTE:

My parents love to serve crushed lingonberries alongside this pie. If you can't find lingonberries, use crushed cranberries instead: You can sweeten them with liquid stevia or powdered erythritol if the tartness of plain cranberries is too much for you.

Five-Ingredient Salmon Dill Quiche

It's easy to make a scrumptious, healthy quiche for tonight's dinner: All you need is five basic ingredients. And the result is a hot, flavorful meal that's bursting with fresh herbs and healthy fats. This quiche is crust-free, but if you'd like to include one, just prepare a batch of Vegan Sugar-Free, Starch-Free Pie Crust (page 28) and prebake it for fifteen minutes before adding the filling.

1½ cups (200 g) finely flaked smoked salmon or lox

1 cup (240 ml) heavy cream

4 eggs

¼ cup (20 g) finely chopped fresh dill

Unrefined sea salt or Himalayan salt, to taste

2 cups (145 g) shredded Swiss cheese or other sharp cheese

—
Yield: 8 to 12 servings

Preheat the oven to 350°F (175°C). Combine the salmon, heavy cream, eggs, and dill in a large bowl. Season with salt. Whisk well and then pour the mixture into a 10-inch (25 cm) pie pan. Spread the shredded cheese evenly on top and bake in the preheated oven for 25 minutes, or until the cheese is melted, golden brown, and bubbly. Remove from the oven, let set 5 minutes, and serve. Store leftovers in an airtight container in the fridge for two to three days.

NUTRITION INFO

WITHOUT CRUST

IN TOTAL:

| 123.7 G PROTEIN |
| 156.6 G FAT |
| 7.9 G NET CARBS |
| 1936 KCAL |

PER SLICE,
IF 8 SLICES IN TOTAL:

| 15.5 G PROTEIN |
| 19.6 G FAT |
| 1.0 G NET CARBS |
| 242 KCAL |

PER SLICE,
IF 12 SLICES IN TOTAL:

| 10.3 G PROTEIN |
| 13.1 G FAT |
| 0.7 G NET CARBS |
| 161 KCAL |

Fabulous Pizza Focaccia for the Whole Family

When you're using starch-free real-food ingredients, a little bit goes a long way. And this pizza focaccia is proof: Just a small slice is sure to fill you up. This is a basic version, so go ahead and pretty it up with more toppings of your choice, such as ham, salami, pepperoni, bell pepper, olives, or sliced tomatoes. You can also replace the dried oregano with fresh basil leaves, but do add them after baking, as basil loses its taste if baked or dried.

FOR THE FOCACCIA CRUST:

2 cups (230 g) almond flour

¼ cup (20 g) unflavored grass-fed whey protein

¼ cup (25 g) egg white protein

2 teaspoons aluminum-free baking powder

1 teaspoon unrefined sea salt or Himalayan salt, or to taste

4 eggs

¼ cup (60 ml) light olive oil

OTHER INGREDIENTS:

½ cup (120 ml) sugar-free pizza sauce

3 cups (300 g) shredded mozzarella cheese

1 tablespoon (3 g) dried oregano

—

Yield: 4 to 6 servings

Preheat the oven to 350°F (175°C). Line a baking sheet with parchment paper.

First, prepare the crust. Place the almond flour, whey protein, egg white protein, baking powder, and salt in a medium bowl. Mix well and set aside.

Place the eggs and the olive oil in a large bowl. Beat with an electric mixer until smooth, about 1 minute. Add the dry ingredients and mix again until smooth, about 1 minute. Pour the batter on the lined baking sheet and spread into a ⅓-inch (8.5 mm) thick layer. Prebake for 10 minutes.

When done, remove the crust from the oven and spread the pizza sauce evenly over it. Top with the cheese and oregano. Bake for 15 minutes, or until the cheese is bubbly and golden brown. Cut into pieces and serve immediately.

VARIATION: For the ultimate focaccia, make the focaccia crust and spread it on the baking sheet as directed. But before baking, brush the surface with extra-virgin olive oil, sprinkle with fresh rosemary needles and sea salt, and bake as directed. Superb!

TIP:

Can't find egg white protein? No problem: Use only whey protein, and increase the amount to ½ cup (40 g).

Five-Ingredient Roasted Mackerel with Thyme and Lemon

Since it's packed with heart-healthy omega-3 fats, mackerel is one of the most nutritious types of fish on the market. It tastes heavenly when it's roasted in the oven, as in this simple recipe. Serve it with lemon wedges, as their bright, sharp acidity contrasts so well with the hot, oily fish.

4 small (about ½ pound, or 230 g, each) or 2 large (about 1 pound, or 450 g, each) whole mackerels, gutted and cleaned

2 teaspoons unrefined sea salt or Himalayan salt

2 tablespoons (28 ml) extra-virgin olive oil

2 organic lemons: 1 sliced, 1 cut into wedges

40 sprigs fresh thyme

—
Yield: 4 servings

Preheat the oven to 400°F (200°C). Make 4 slashes to each side of the mackerel with a sharp knife. Rub the mackerel with salt and olive oil both inside and outside. Stuff the mackerels with the lemon slices and thyme sprigs. For small mackerel, use five thyme sprigs per mackerel; for large ones, use ten sprigs.

Place the fish on a roasting pan and roast for 25 minutes, or until the eyes are white and the fish flakes easily with a fork. Don't overbake, as the fish dries out quickly.

While the fish is roasting, remove the leaves from the rest of the thyme sprigs. Discard the stems. When the fish is done, remove it from the oven and serve sprinkled with the thyme leaves and garnished with the lemon wedges.

NUTRITION INFO

IN TOTAL:

191.2 G PROTEIN

59.5 G FAT

0.4 G NET CARBS

1302 KCAL

PER SERVING,
IF 4 SERVINGS IN TOTAL:

47.8 G PROTEIN

14.9 G FAT

0.1 G NET CARBS

326 KCAL

Better than Macaroni and Cheese

Looking for filling, low-sugar comfort food your whole family will love? Here's the answer. This creamy, starch-free main is perfect for chilly winter evenings—or whenever you need the dinnertime equivalent of a warm blanket and a hug. It's highly tummy-friendly, too, since it replaces wheat-filled pasta with oh-so-nutritious cauliflower. And that means it won't spike your blood sugar. What's not to like?

1 cup (240 ml) heavy cream

2 eggs

1 teaspoon unrefined sea salt or Himalayan salt, or to taste

2 teaspoons dry mustard (that is, mustard powder or ground mustard seeds)

½ teaspoon onion powder

¼ teaspoon garlic powder

2 cups (190 g) shredded cheddar cheese

4 cups (565 g) precooked (crisp), cauliflower, chopped into ¼-inch (6 mm) chunks

1 cup (100 g) shredded mozzarella cheese

¼ cup (30 g) almond flour

—
Yield: 6 servings

Preheat the oven to 400°F (200°C).

Combine the cream, eggs, salt, mustard, onion powder, and garlic powder in a large saucepan. Heat over medium heat, constantly and carefully stirring with a wire whisk until the mixture starts to thicken. When this happens, reduce the heat to a minimum and add 1½ cups (143 g) of the cheddar cheese. Mix until all the cheese is melted, then add the cauliflower and mix well again.

Transfer the mixture to a greased baking dish. Sprinkle the remaining cheddar cheese, all the mozzarella cheese, and the almond flour evenly on top. Bake for 25 minutes, until the top is golden brown and the cheese is bubbly. Let stand for 10 minutes and then serve.

NUTRITION INFO

IN TOTAL:

119.6 G PROTEIN
204.6 G FAT
23.1 G NET CARBS
2412 KCAL

PER SERVING,
IF 6 SERVINGS IN TOTAL:

19.9 G PROTEIN
34.1 G FAT
3.8 G NET CARBS
402 KCAL

Five-Ingredient Mozzarella Chicken Wings

I've done plenty of experimenting with recipes for chicken wings, and this one is definitely the winner. It's a bit messy to eat—but that's half the fun, of course. This version is kid-friendly, so it isn't spicy, but if you want to kick up the heat, go ahead and add a little cayenne pepper. If you're expecting guests, these wings make great appetizers, too. (Just be sure to provide extra napkins!)

1½ pounds (680 g) chicken wings

¼ cup (60 ml) light olive oil

7 ounces (200 g) shredded mozzarella cheese

2 teaspoons onion powder

2 teaspoons paprika

1 teaspoon unrefined sea salt or Himalayan salt, or to taste

—
Yield: 4 servings

Preheat the oven to 450°F (230°C).

Place the chicken wings and the oil in a large bowl and toss well. Place the oiled chicken wings in a large glass or ceramic baking dish. If there's any oil left in the bowl, pour it over the chicken.

Place the mozzarella, onion powder, paprika, and salt, in a medium bowl. Mix well. Sprinkle the mozzarella mixture evenly on the chicken wings and bake for 15 to 20 minutes, or until the juices run clear. Enjoy hot—but don't burn yourself!

NUTRITION INFO

IN TOTAL:

170.6 G PROTEIN

173.1 G FAT

1.2 G NET CARBS

2245 KCAL

PER SERVING,
IF 4 SERVINGS IN TOTAL:

42.6 G PROTEIN

43.3 G FAT

0.3 G NET CARBS

561 KCAL

Starch-Free Wiener Schnitzels

This one's a real European classic—but my gluten-free, starch-free version is so much healthier than the original. (Feel free to make a batch of the breading mixture and keep it on hand as a pantry staple to use for breading chicken, fish, veggies, or cheese. The possibilities are endless!) Serve these schnitzels garnished with anchovies, capers, and lemon slices, plus some oven-baked turnip or rutabaga fries on the side.

For the breading mixture:

1 cup (115 g) almond flour

1 tablespoon (9 g) psyllium husk powder

1 teaspoon onion powder

1 teaspoon unrefined sea salt
or Himalayan salt

1 pinch ground white pepper

Other ingredients:

2 eggs

4 veal medallions, pork chops, or chicken breasts (12 ounces, or 340 g, in total)

1 stick (8 tablespoons [4 ounces], or 115 g) grass-fed butter or lard, for frying

—
Yield: 4 servings

Combine the ingredients for the breading in a shallow bowl. Set aside.

Place the eggs in a separate shallow bowl and mix gently with a fork. Set aside.

Pound the meat into ¼-inch (6 mm) thick cutlets, working from the center of the meat outward.

Heat a skillet over medium-high heat and add the butter. Take one cutlet and dip it in the egg so that it's completely covered. Then dip it immediately into the breading mixture so that it's completely covered. (You can gently press the breading into the cutlet to help it stick.) Place the breaded cutlet in the skillet and fry until cooked through and golden brown, approximately 4 minutes per side. Flip only once during cooking.

Repeat this process with the rest of the cutlets and serve immediately, with turnip or rutabaga fries.

NUTRITION INFO

IN TOTAL:	
150.3 G PROTEIN	
203.7 G FAT	
9.6 G NET CARBS	
2473 KCAL	
PER SERVING, IF 4 SERVINGS IN TOTAL:	
37.6 G PROTEIN	
50.9 G FAT	
2.4 G NET CARBS	
618 KCAL	

Skinny Tuna Pasta with Shirataki Noodles

You're starving, and you're just cooking for one tonight. What to do? Skip processed convenience foods, and treat yourself to this fresh, light tuna pasta instead. It's both protein-rich and packed with vegetables, and it's very low-starch, thanks to the shirataki noodles, which are virtually calorie-free. And a final squeeze of fresh lemon juice plus a scattering of fiery red pepper flakes really put a spring in its step.

2.9-ounce (80 g) can tuna in olive oil, not drained

½ small onion, finely chopped

1 clove garlic, crushed

2 sun-dried tomato halves, finely chopped

4 medium canned, drained artichoke hearts, chopped

1 package (7 ounces, or 200 g) shirataki pasta of your preferred shape, rinsed and drained

½ teaspoon unrefined sea salt or Himalayan salt, or to taste

2 teaspoons freshly squeezed lemon juice

1 tablespoon (15 ml) extra-virgin olive oil

Red pepper flakes, to taste

—
Yield: 1 serving

Drain the tuna and reserve the oil. Heat a skillet over medium-high heat. (Avoid high heat, as it encourages the olive oil to splatter.) Add the olive oil from the drained tuna, plus the onion, garlic, sun-dried tomatoes, and the artichoke hearts. Cook, stirring occasionally, until the onion is translucent, about 5 minutes.

Add the shirataki pasta and the salt and stir well. Then add the tuna, mix gently, and heat until piping hot, but don't cook. Place on a serving plate, drizzle with the lemon juice and the olive oil, and top with the red pepper flakes. Serve immediately.

NUTRITION INFO

IN TOTAL:

16.1 G PROTEIN

47.7 G FAT

6.7 G NET CARBS

524 KCAL

Quick Chicken Fajita Pasta

Craving the flavors of chicken fajitas, minus the carbs and sugar? Amazingly, this creamy, spiced pasta is both starch- and dairy-free, and it's a snap to make, because it relies on just a handful of store-cupboard staples. If you can't find shirataki pasta, replace it with zoodles (that is, spiralized zucchini). Either way, it's a weeknight winner.

2 tablespoons (28 ml) light olive oil

2 teaspoons homemade fajita seasoning mix (see sidebar)

½ small onion, finely chopped

1 garlic clove, finely chopped

½ green bell pepper, chopped

4 ounces (115 g) chicken breast, chopped into bite-size pieces

1 tablespoon (16 g) unsweetened tomato paste

¼ cup (60 ml) coconut cream

1 package (7 ounces, or 200 g) shirataki pasta (fettucine-style, if possible), rinsed and drained

Unrefined sea salt or Himalayan salt and freshly ground black pepper, to taste

—
Yield: 1 serving

Heat a skillet over medium-high heat. Add the olive oil, fajita seasoning, onion, and garlic. Mix well and cook until the onion is translucent, approximately 5 minutes. Add the bell pepper and the chicken breast. Cook, stirring constantly, until the chicken is done and the juices run clear. Then add the tomato paste and coconut cream and cook until the sauce is as thick as you like it (the longer the sauce cooks, the thicker it gets). Add the shirataki pasta and mix well. Heat it through, but don't cook. Season with salt and pepper and serve immediately.

NUTRITION INFO

IN TOTAL:

30.9 G PROTEIN

44.3 G FAT

7.0 G NET CARBS

536 KCAL

HOMEMADE FAJITA SEASONING

1 teaspoon onion powder

1 teaspoon ground cumin

1 teaspoon paprika

½ teaspoon garlic powder

¼ teaspoon cayenne pepper

Mix all the spices together well and store in an airtight container.

The Easiest Spaghetti Bolognese

Spaghetti Bolognese is a classic comfort food, beloved especially by kids. But starchy spaghetti can raise the roof on your blood sugar levels—and that's never a good thing. Your veins and brains will thank you when you make this low-sugar version, though. It's criminally easy, too, so whip up a batch the next time you need to feed the whole family fast.

FOR THE BOLOGNESE SAUCE:

Oil or butter for frying

2 pounds (910 g) ground beef

3 cups (710 ml) unsweetened tomato sauce

1 tablespoon (3 g) dried oregano

2 teaspoons onion powder

½ teaspoon garlic powder

1 teaspoon unrefined sea salt or Himalayan salt, or to taste

Freshly ground black pepper, to taste

OTHER INGREDIENTS:

2 packages (7 ounces, or 200 g, each) shirataki spaghetti

1 ounce (30 g) Parmesan cheese

Yield: 4 servings

Heat a skillet over medium-high heat. Add the butter or oil and let melt. Add the ground beef and cook, crumbling the meat with the back of your spoon or spatula as you do so. When the meat is done, add the tomato sauce, oregano, onion powder, and garlic powder. Cook, uncovered, until the sauce is reduced and thick. (Lower the heat if the sauce is about to spill over.) Season with salt and pepper.

Prepare the shirataki spaghetti according to the package instructions. Divide the spaghetti among four serving plates, and top each with the Bolognese sauce. Grate some Parmesan on top of each serving and serve immediately.

NUTRITION INFO

IN TOTAL:	
186.6 G PROTEIN	
104.9 G FAT	
32.6 G NET CARBS	
1822 KCAL	

PER SERVING, IF 4 SERVINGS IN TOTAL:	
46.7 G PROTEIN	
26.2 G FAT	
8.1 G NET CARBS	
456 KCAL	

TIP:

Try different starch-free spaghettis. For instance, instead of shirataki, you can use zoodles. They're a good match for Bolognese, because they taste especially crunchy and fresh.

Easy Cauli Rice Mushroom and Parmesan Risotto

Traditional risotto has two major drawbacks: It requires time and skill to perfect, and the starchy arborio rice from which it's made isn't very healthy. This version is both good for you and easy to make. Don't be put off by the nutritional yeast; it's a natural, nutrient-rich flavor enhancer that adds a cheesy taste to dishes. If you don't have any, add another ¼ cup (20 g) of grated Parmesan.

2 tablespoons (1 ounce, or 30 g) grass-fed butter

4 cups (280 g) button mushrooms, chopped

½ cup (120 ml) chicken stock or vegetable stock

¼ cup (60 ml) dry white wine

1 tablespoon (5 g) nutritional yeast

1 teaspoon onion powder

¼ teaspoon garlic powder

4 cups (450 g) cauliflower rice

¾ cup plus ¼ cup (60 g plus 20 g) freshly grated Parmesan cheese, divided

½ teaspoon unrefined sea salt or Himalayan salt, or to taste

Pinch freshly ground white pepper

—
Yield: 2 to 4 servings

Heat a large skillet over medium-high heat and melt the butter in it. Add the mushrooms and cook, stirring occasionally, until all the liquid has evaporated and the mushrooms are tender. Then add the chicken stock, white wine, nutritional yeast, onion powder, and garlic powder and cook, uncovered, until the liquid has reduced by half.

Now add the cauliflower and cook, stirring constantly, until crisp-tender, about 5 minutes. Add ¾ cup (60 g) Parmesan and stir until melted. Season with salt and white pepper.

Divide the risotto between two serving plates and sprinkle the remaining Parmesan on top of each serving. Serve immediately.

VARIATION: Want to make this dish even more satisfying? Add 1 cup (140 g) cooked and cubed chicken along with the cauliflower.

NUTRITION INFO

IN TOTAL:

43.7 G PROTEIN	
48.6 G FAT	
12.6 G NET CARBS	
702 KCAL	

PER SERVING, IF 2 SERVINGS IN TOTAL:	PER SERVING, IF 4 SERVINGS IN TOTAL:
21.9 G PROTEIN	10.9 G PROTEIN
24.3 G FAT	12.1 G FAT
6.3 G NET CARBS	3.2 G NET CARBS
351 KCAL	176 KCAL

Vegetarian Eggplant Curry with Cauli Basmati Rice

A veritable kaleidoscope of tastes and textures, this dish contrasts soft, tender eggplant with crisp fennel and crunchy celery, all bathed in a coconutty cream sauce. Partner it with a batch of Cauli Basmati Rice, a healthy version of traditional, starch-filled basmati rice and an ideal match for all sorts of Asian dishes, such as curries and stir-fries.

FOR THE VEGETARIAN EGGPLANT CURRY:

Oil or butter for frying

1 to 2 tablespoons (15 to 30 g) green Thai curry paste

1 small onion, chopped

13.5-ounce (400 ml) can coconut milk

1 medium eggplant, diced

1 small fennel bulb, shredded

2 celery stalks, sliced into ¼-inch (6 mm) slices

2 tablespoons (28 ml) fish sauce

1 tablespoon (15 ml) freshly squeezed lime juice

1 tablespoon (10 g) erythritol-based brown sugar substitute (optional)

FOR THE CAULI BASMATI RICE:

1 pound (450 g) cauliflower

1 teaspoon cumin seeds

2 tablespoons (1 ounce, or 30 g) grass-fed butter or olive oil

⅓ cup (60 g) frozen green peas

Unrefined sea salt or Himalayan salt, to taste

—
Yield: 4 servings

Prepare the Vegetarian Eggplant Curry. Place a skillet over medium heat. Add the oil or butter and let it get hot. Add the curry paste and heat for 30 seconds, constantly stirring. Add the onion and cook, stirring occasionally, until translucent, about 5 minutes. (Reduce the heat if the onion is about to brown.)

Add the coconut milk and bring to a boil and then add the eggplant to the skillet. Cook, covered, for 10 minutes or until tender. (Hint: While the eggplant is cooking, you can start preparing the Cauli Basmati Rice. See step 4.)

Add the fennel and the celery to the skillet. Cook, uncovered, for 5 minutes or until crisp-tender. Add the fish sauce, lime juice, and sweetener, if using, and cook, uncovered, for 1 minute. Remove from the heat and serve with Cauli Basmati Rice.

Prepare the Cauli Basmati Rice. Process the cauliflower in a food processor until a ricelike consistency is achieved.

TIP:

Not a fan of fennel? Don't worry! Its taste is very mild and subtle in this dish. But feel free to replace the fennel or celery with other nonstarchy vegetables such as zucchini, squash, green bell pepper, carrot matchsticks, or shredded cabbage, if you like.

Heat a skillet over high heat. Add the cumin seeds and heat for 30 seconds until fragrant, stirring all the time. (Don't let the seeds burn.) Set aside.

Reduce the heat to medium-low. Melt the butter (or add the oil) in the skillet and then add the cauliflower. Mix well so that the cauliflower is completely coated. Cover and let simmer for 5 to 10 minutes, or until the cauliflower is crisp-tender. (Don't let it get too soft.) If it starts to brown, add a tablespoon or two (15 to 28 ml) of water and mix well. Add the peas and mix well. Season with salt. Let stand, covered, until the peas have defrosted and are warmed through. Mix well and serve immediately with Vegetarian Eggplant Curry, above.

NUTRITION INFO

IN TOTAL:

38.8 G PROTEIN

112.1 G FAT

54.6 G NET CARBS

1383 KCAL

PER SERVING,
IF 4 SERVINGS IN TOTAL:

9.7 G PROTEIN

28.0 G FAT

13.7 G NET CARBS

346 KCAL

FOR THE VEGETARIAN EGGPLANT CURRY

IN TOTAL:

26.9 G PROTEIN

86.4 G FAT

38.8 G NET CARBS

1039 KCAL

PER SERVING,
IF 4 SERVINGS IN TOTAL:

6.7 G PROTEIN

21.6 G FAT

9.7 G NET CARBS

260 KCAL

FOR THE CAULI BASMATI RICE

IN TOTAL:

11.9 G PROTEIN

25.7 G FAT

15.8 G NET CARBS

344 KCAL

PER SERVING,
IF 4 SERVINGS IN TOTAL:

3.0 G PROTEIN

6.4 G FAT

4.0 G NET CARBS

86 KCAL

Cauli Rice Seafood Paella

You don't have to give up Spanish-style paella just because you're eating low-sugar. This version replaces the rice with cauli rice, but it's just as good—and it's an entire meal in a single skillet. There are as many recipes for paella as there are cooks, so each one is unique. This is my favorite, but feel free to tweak it to your taste. For instance, my family and I love smoked paprika's distinct flavor, but you can omit it, or replace it with regular paprika, if you're not a fan.

2 tablespoons (28 ml) extra-virgin olive oil

1 medium onion, chopped

4 garlic cloves, crushed

1 large red bell pepper, chopped

8 saffron threads

4 cups (450 g) cauliflower rice

½ cup (120 ml) chicken stock or fish stock

2 tablespoons (32 g) tomato paste

½ teaspoon smoked paprika

½ cup (90 g) frozen green peas

1 pound (450 g) frozen precooked seafood mix

1 teaspoon unrefined sea salt or Himalayan salt, or to taste

Pinch cayenne pepper

—
Yield: 2 to 4 servings

Heat a large skillet over medium-high heat. Add the olive oil, onion, garlic, bell pepper, and saffron. Cook, stirring, until the vegetables are crisp-tender, about 5 minutes. Then add the cauliflower, stock, tomato paste, and smoked paprika and cook, covered, until the cauliflower is crisp-tender, about 5 minutes.

Add the frozen peas and the frozen seafood mix. Heat, stirring, until defrosted and completely hot, about 5 to 10 minutes. (Don't cook the seafood or it will become tough.) Season with salt and cayenne pepper and serve immediately.

VARIATION: Serve this with mussels, as shown opposite. Rinse and steam them and add just before serving. If you're not a seafood eater, use 1 pound (450 g) cooked and cubed chicken instead of the seafood mix. Or use the same amount of chorizo sausage, or a mix of chorizo and chicken. (Fry the sausage before adding it.)

NUTRITION INFO

IN TOTAL:

78.7 G PROTEIN	
35.6 G FAT	
44.0 G NET CARBS	
813 KCAL	

PER SERVING, IF 2 SERVINGS IN TOTAL:	PER SERVING, IF 4 SERVINGS IN TOTAL:
39.3 G PROTEIN	19.7 G PROTEIN
17.8 G FAT	8.9 G FAT
22.0 G NET CARBS	11.0 G NET CARBS
406 KCAL	203 KCAL

TIP:
Don't want to spend money on pricey saffron? Use ¼ teaspoon turmeric instead. You'll get the same rich yellow color, and plenty of health benefits, too, as turmeric is said to have antioxidant and anti-inflammatory properties.

Tasty Taco Casserole

Ever checked the ingredient list on that packet of store-bought taco seasoning? Lots of them are full of sugar and starch, so they're off-limits if you're eating low-sugar. But when you make your own homemade taco seasoning—with just five ingredients!—you can be sure that it's clean and sugar-free. It's ideal in this punchy, cheesy, kid-friendly casserole.

FOR THE TACO SEASONING:

2 tablespoons (15 g) chili powder

1½ tablespoons (11 g) ground cumin

1½ teaspoons onion powder

1 teaspoon garlic powder

½ teaspoon dried oregano

OTHER INGREDIENTS:

Oil or butter for frying

2 pounds (910 g) ground beef

15-ounce (425 g) can green beans, drained

16-ounce (450 g) can diced tomatoes

2 teaspoons unrefined sea salt or Himalayan salt, or to taste

6 cups (240 g) cubed Easy Fluffy Bread (page 24)

4 cups (380 g) shredded mild cheddar cheese

—
Yield: 8 servings

Place all taco seasoning ingredients into a small jar with a tightly fitting lid. Close the lid, and shake until well mixed.

Prepare the meat sauce. Heat a large skillet over medium-high heat. Add the oil or butter. When hot, add the ground beef and cook. When the meat is browned, add the taco seasoning, green beans, and diced tomatoes. Mix well. Reduce the heat to low, and let simmer until the sauce has thickened, about 20 minutes. Season with salt, mix well, and set aside.

Preheat the oven to 350°F (175 °C). Lay half of the bread cubes evenly in the bottom of a casserole dish. Spread half of the meat sauce on the bread cubes and sprinkle half of the cheese on the meat sauce. Spread the rest of the bread cubes on the cheese, top with the rest of the meat sauce, and, finally, sprinkle the rest of the cheese on top. Bake for 30 minutes, or until the cheese is bubbly and golden brown. Remove from the oven, let stand for 10 minutes, and serve.

VARIATION: You can also use half a batch of Just Like Tortilla Chips (page 102) in place of the bread cubes.

NUTRITION INFO

IN TOTAL:	
313.4 G PROTEIN	
283.4 G FAT	
33.7 G NET CARBS	
3954 KCAL	
PER SERVING, IF 8 SERVINGS IN TOTAL:	
39.2 G PROTEIN	
35.4 G FAT	
4.2 G NET CARBS	
494 KCAL	

TIP:

The taco seasoning is a little spicy. If you're making this dish for kids, you can replace 1 tablespoon (7 g) of the chili powder with paprika.

CHAPTER 5

Snacks

Even if you eat three meals a day, hunger can strike when you least expect it. Long, hard days at work or school take their toll on grownups, leading to rumbling bellies and flagging energy levels. And kids, with their little tummies, can't eat huge portions all at once, so they need healthy snacks, too. In the coming pages, you'll find ideas for low-sugar snacks that are convenient for noshing on the go—or for leaving in the fridge for your child to grab after school.

Just Like Tortilla Chips

Ditch the starchy corn and the food additives. You don't need them to make "tortilla" chips that will satisfy your craving for a crunchy, salty snack. This version is bursting with healthy ingredients and lots of fiber, plus—thanks to the nutritional yeast and the onion powder—plenty of flavor. Try dipping them in a batch of homemade guacamole.

8 ounces (230 g) blanched almonds

¼ cup (45 g) white chia seeds

1 tablespoon (5 g) nutritional yeast

1 teaspoon onion powder

1 teaspoon unrefined sea salt
or Himalayan salt, or to taste

2 ounces (60 g) full-fat
cream cheese, softened

—
Yield: about 48 chips

Preheat the oven to 210°F (100°C). Place the almonds, chia seeds, nutritional yeast, onion powder, and salt in a food processor. Process until the mixture resembles corn meal.

Transfer the mixture to a medium bowl. Add the cream cheese and knead until a smooth dough forms. If you can't form the dough into a ball, add more cream cheese.

Place the dough on a baking sheet lined with parchment paper. Place another piece of parchment paper on the dough. Using a rolling pin, roll the dough out as thinly as possible. Remove the top piece of parchment paper.

Cut the dough with a knife or pizza cutter into squares and then crosswise into triangles. Place in the oven and bake for 50 to 60 minutes, checking frequently to prevent the chips from becoming too dark or burning.

Let cool completely, then break into triangles along the precut lines. Store in an airtight container in a cool, dry place for up to one week.

NUTRITION INFO

IN TOTAL:

| 65.0 G PROTEIN |
| 143.4 G FAT |
| 27.1 G NET CARBS |
| 1662 KCAL |

PER CHIP,
IF 48 CHIPS IN TOTAL:

| 1.4 G PROTEIN |
| 3.0 G FAT |
| 0.6 G NET CARBS |
| 35 KCAL |

Magic Cauliflower Popcorn

Packed with fiber and vitamin C, this cauliflower "popcorn" beats the traditional starch-bomb version in every way. And best of all, it takes just five simple items! There's a magic ingredient at work here, of course: cheddar cheese powder, which makes this popcorn incredibly tasty and impossible to resist. Don't bake the cauliflower for too long, though, as you want to be sure to retain its delicious crunch.

2 pounds (910 g) cauliflower (about 1 large head), chopped into bite-size pieces

1 tablespoon (15 ml) light olive oil

1 teaspoon unrefined sea salt, or to taste

¼ teaspoon garlic powder

⅓ cup (35 g) white cheddar cheese powder

—
Yield: about 5 cups (500 g)

Preheat the oven to 400°F (200°C). Line a baking sheet with parchment paper. Place the cauliflower, olive oil, salt, and garlic powder in a large bowl. Toss until well mixed.

Spread the cauliflower on the lined baking sheet in a single layer so that the cauliflower pieces barely touch one other, and bake for 10 minutes.

Remove the cauliflower from the oven and pour the hot cauliflower pieces into a large heatproof bowl. (The best way to do this is by grabbing the short ends of the cauliflower-loaded parchment paper and carefully lifting it up to pour the cauliflower right into the bowl. Don't burn yourself!) Add the cheddar cheese powder and toss with a spoon until the cauliflower is completely and evenly covered. Let cool on a cooling rack for a few minutes. Serve warm.

NUTRITION INFO

IN TOTAL:

30.3 G PROTEIN	
26.0 G FAT	
27.0 G NET CARBS	
463 KCAL	

PER 1 CUP (100 G):

6.1 G PROTEIN	
5.2 G FAT	
5.4 G NET CARBS	
93 KCAL	

Easy Broccoli "Tater Tots"

Did you know that just 3½ ounces (100 g) of commercially produced Tater Tots contain about eight sugar cubes? So, if you wouldn't feed your child eight sugar cubes (especially at a single sitting), skip them and make a batch of these addictive-but-nutritious Easy Broccoli "Tater Tots" instead. They're just as good, and far healthier, since there's no nasty sugar in sight.

1 cup (240 g) soft-cooked broccoli, tightly packed

1 cup (100 g) grated mozzarella cheese

½ cup (60 g) almond flour

1 teaspoon psyllium husk powder

1 teaspoon onion powder

1 egg

1 teaspoon unrefined sea salt or Himalayan salt, or to taste

2 tablespoons (28 ml) extra-light olive oil, for brushing

—
Yield: about 16 tater tots

Preheat the oven to 350°F (175 °C). Line a baking sheet with parchment paper. Place all ingredients in a medium bowl and mix with an electric mixer until smooth.

Scoop up 2 tablespoons (28 g) of the mixture. With liberally oiled hands, shape it into a cylindrical or rectangular tater-tot shape. Place the tater tot on the lined baking sheet. Repeat with the remaining broccoli mixture.

Brush each tater tot generously with olive oil, then transfer the tray to the oven and bake for 20 minutes, or until golden brown. (Keep an eye on them to prevent them from burning.) Remove from the oven, let cool, and then serve with Five-Ingredient Sugar-Free Ketchup (page 10), Foolproof One-Minute Mayo (page 12), or a sugar-free dip of your choice.

NUTRITION INFO

IN TOTAL:

56.7 G PROTEIN	
84.0 G FAT	
11.4 G NET CARBS	
1043 KCAL	

PER TATER TOT,
IF 16 TATER TOTS IN TOTAL:

3.5 G PROTEIN	
5.2 G FAT	
0.7 G NET CARBS	
65 KCAL	

Best BBQ Nuts

These nuts make a great party snack, or an impromptu appetizer for last-minute guests. Don't be surprised, though, if these gems disappear as soon as you serve them, since they're spiced, crunchy, and finger-licking good. During the holidays, you can fill a beautiful glass jar with these nuts and give them as a healthy, delicious gift. Feel free to mix things up by experimenting with different herbs and spices.

8 ounces (230 g) mixed nuts
(such as almonds, blanched hazelnuts, pecans, or macadamia nuts)

1 tablespoon (15 ml) extra-light olive oil

1½ teaspoons salt-free
barbecue seasoning

1 teaspoon unrefined sea salt
or Himalayan salt, or to taste

1 tablespoon (10 g) erythritol-based
brown sugar substitute (optional)

—
Yield: about 2½ cups (350 g)

Preheat the oven to 350°F (175 °C). Line a baking sheet with parchment paper. Place all the ingredients into a resealable freezer bag. Close the bag tightly and shake it well to let the spices and oil cover the nuts evenly. Spread the mixture over the baking sheet into a thin, even layer. Bake for 10 to 12 minutes, or until golden brown. Keep an eye on the nuts as they bake, as they burn very easily.

Let the nuts cool completely on the baking sheet and then remove and serve. Store leftovers in an airtight container in a cool, dry place for up to two days.

NUTRITION INFO

*NOTE: THE EXACT VALUES
DEPEND ON THE NUT MIX USED.*

IN TOTAL:

34.2 G PROTEIN	
162.2 G FAT	
32.2 G NET CARBS	
1757 KCAL	

PER ¼ CUP (ABOUT 35 G):

8.6 G PROTEIN	
40.5 G FAT	
8.0 G NET CARBS	
439 KCAL	

Two-Ingredient Crackers

These melt-in-your-mouth crackers are such a healthy alternative to starch-laden store-bought crackers or potato chips. With just two ingredients, they're amazingly simple. They're great on their own, or with just about any kind of low-sugar topping. Try spreading them with flavored cream cheeses (as long as they're made without food additives, of course). Or you can add chopped fresh chives to the dough to make cream cheese and chive crackers.

2 cups (230 g) almond flour

2.5 ounces (70 g) full-fat cream cheese (any flavor)

1 teaspoon unrefined sea salt or Himalayan salt, or to taste (optional)

—

Yield: about 48 crackers

Preheat the oven to 210°F (100°C). Mix all ingredients by hand in a medium bowl. Knead for about half a minute or until a smooth dough forms.

Place the dough on a baking sheet lined with parchment paper. Place another piece of parchment paper on top of the dough. Using a rolling pin, roll the dough out as thinly as possible between the two pieces of parchment paper. Then remove the top piece.

Use a knife or pizza cutter to cut the dough into squares (or other shapes of your choice). Place in the oven and bake for 50 to 60 minutes, checking frequently to prevent the crackers from becoming too dark or burning. Let cool completely before removing from the baking sheet. Store in an airtight container in a cool, dry place for up to one week.

NUTRITION INFO

IN TOTAL:

54.0 G PROTEIN	
131.8 G FAT	
23.9 G NET CARBS	
1498 KCAL	

PER CRACKER,
IF 48 CRACKERS IN TOTAL:

1.1 G PROTEIN	
2.7 G FAT	
0.5 G NET CARBS	
31 KCAL	

Cinnamon Roll–Flavored Apple Chips

Finally: There's a healthy way to enjoy cinnamon buns! And the proof's in the pudding—or, in this case, in the Cinnamon Roll–Flavored Apple Chips. Choose the sourest possible apples for the lowest sugar content, then rub them with spices and sweetener and pop them into a warm oven for a few hours. You can get creative with your choice of spices, too. For example, pumpkin pie spice makes a great autumnal treat, and gingerbread seasoning is perfect for the holidays. Don't despair if the chips aren't crisp when they're warm from the oven: Thanks to the erythritol, they'll crisp up after cooling down.

2 tablespoons (16 g) powdered erythritol

½ teaspoon Ceylon cinnamon

¼ teaspoon vanilla powder

2 small Granny Smith apples, or other sour apples

—

Yield: about 3½ cups (98 g)

NUTRITION INFO

IN TOTAL:	
0.7 G PROTEIN	
0.3 G FAT	
23.6 G NET CARBS	
105 KCAL	
PER 1 CUP (28 G):	
0.2 G PROTEIN	
0.1 G FAT	
5.9 G NET CARBS	
26 KCAL	

Preheat the oven to 200°F (90°C). Line two baking sheets with parchment paper. Place the erythritol, cinnamon, and vanilla powder in a small bowl and mix well.

Slice the apples as thinly as possible. Discard the seeds.

Place the apple slices on the lined baking sheets in a single layer. Using clean hands, rub each slice on both sides with the sweetener-and-spice mixture. Then bake for 4 hours or until crisp, switching the position of the baking sheets halfway through baking. When the slices are crisp, remove the baking sheets. Let the chips cool and then serve. Store leftovers in an airtight container for up to two weeks.

TIP:

To make a sweetener-free version, just rub the apple slices with a mixture of cinnamon and vanilla powder.

NOTE:

Got leftover sweetener-and-spice mixture? Don't let it go to waste: Sprinkle it on your breakfast yogurt, or spread butter on a slice of Easy Fluffy Bread (page 24) and top it with the sweetener-and-spice mixture, to make instant cinnamon toast.

CHAPTER 6

Desserts

Quitting sugar doesn't mean saying no to dessert. You can still enjoy decadent-tasting sweet treats on a low-sugar lifestyle—except that these versions are actually good for you. Made with natural sweeteners and clean ingredients, the luscious recipes in this chapter are safe for kids and adults alike.

Easy Sugar-Free Vanilla Ice Cream

This no-cook recipe makes homemade sugar-free ice cream ridiculously simple. And it's extra-creamy, thanks to a secret ingredient—full-fat sour cream—which also adds a palate-pleasing tang. The hardest part? Waiting for the ice cream to freeze before you dig in. (Please note that this recipe contains raw egg.)

1 egg

⅓ cup (43 g) powdered erythritol

10 drops vanilla stevia, or to taste

1 cup (240 ml) heavy cream

8 ounces (230 g) full-fat sour cream

2 teaspoons vanilla extract, or the scraped seeds from one vanilla bean

—

Yield: 4 servings

Place all ingredients in a deep, narrow bowl. First stir well with a spoon to fold in the powdered erythritol and then mix with an electric mixer until thoroughly combined. Pour the mixture into the ice cream maker and let it churn according to the manufacturer's instructions. Serve it immediately after churning for soft-serve ice cream, but if you prefer a harder ice cream, you can freeze it for an hour or so before serving. Store in the freezer for up to two weeks.

NUTRITION INFO

IN TOTAL:

19.5 G PROTEIN	
130.1 G FAT	
17.8 G NET CARBS	
1320 KCAL	

PER SERVING,
IF 4 SERVINGS IN TOTAL:

4.9 G PROTEIN	
32.5 G FAT	
4.4 G NET CARBS	
330 KCAL	

Quick and Rich Low-Sugar Chocolate Mousse

Having a busy day? No problem: There's still plenty of time to enjoy a sugar-free dessert. Get your chocolate fix with this mouthwatering—and nutritious—chocolate mousse, which takes just a few minutes to prepare. You can eat it right away if you like, or, to help it set, pop it into the fridge for half an hour or so. (Please note that this recipe contains raw egg.)

2 eggs

¼ cup (30 g) unsweetened dark cocoa powder

¼ cup (32 g) powdered erythritol

Pinch unrefined sea salt or Himalayan salt

⅔ cup (160 ml) heavy cream

25 drops vanilla stevia

Rum or sugar-free rum flavoring, to taste (optional)

Grated dark chocolate (with a minimum cocoa content of 85 percent) and whipped cream, to serve

—
Yield: 4 servings

Using an electric mixer, beat the eggs, cocoa powder, erythritol, and salt on high speed until fluffy, about 5 minutes. Add the heavy cream and beat until the mixture reaches a mousse-like consistency, about 5 minutes. Add the vanilla stevia and the rum, if using, and beat until well mixed, about 1 minute. Divide the mousse among four serving bowls and refrigerate for 30 minutes to help it set, if you have time. (If not, go ahead and serve it immediately.) Decorate with grated dark chocolate and whipped cream and serve.

TIP:

Use natural flavorings to add variation to this dessert, such as orange, cherry, or almond. Flavored stevia can do the trick, too, so feel free to experiment.

NUTRITION INFO

IN TOTAL:

24.2 G PROTEIN	
74.0 G FAT	
7.7 G NET CARBS	
799 KCAL	

PER SERVING,
IF 4 SERVINGS IN TOTAL:

6.0 G PROTEIN	
18.5 G FAT	
1.9 G NET CARBS	
200 KCAL	

Five-Ingredient Heaven and Hell Cheesecake

You won't be able to believe that this sinful-tasting cheesecake is actually good for you. But it's true! With only five natural ingredients, it's a fluffy, no-cheat cheesecake that's so easy to make it's practically foolproof—if you follow the instructions, that is. Don't despair if you see a crater in the middle of the cheesecake when it's time to turn off the heat in the oven: The surface of the cake will even out when it's cooling in the oven.

Butter (for greasing)

1 pound (450 g) full-fat cream cheese, softened

½ cup (65 g) powdered erythritol

⅓ cup (80 g) full-fat sour cream, at room temperature

2 eggs, at room temperature

1 teaspoon vanilla extract

—

Yield: 8 servings

Preheat the oven to 300°F (150°C). Grease an 8-inch (20 cm) springform pan generously with butter. Combine the cream cheese, sweetener, and sour cream in a medium bowl. Mix until smooth and fluffy, about 5 minutes. Add the eggs one at a time, beating well after each addition. Add the vanilla extract, beat it until well mixed, and then pour the batter into the pan.

Place a shallow, ovenproof bowl on the lowest rack. Carefully fill it three-quarters full with boiling water. Place the dish with the batter on the middle oven rack.

Bake for 45 minutes, or until the edges are firm but the center is still wobbly. Turn off the heat, but do not remove the cake from the oven: Let it sit in the oven for 1 hour. Remove the cake and let it cool to room temperature before placing it in the fridge for 6 hours or overnight. Bring to room temperature 30 minutes before serving.

NUTRITION INFO

IN TOTAL:

44.1 G PROTEIN	
133.0 G FAT	
18.5 G NET CARBS	
1466 KCAL	

PER SLICE,
IF 8 SLICES IN TOTAL:

5.5 G PROTEIN	
16.6 G FAT	
2.3 G NET CARBS	
183 KCAL	

NOTE:

Don't increase the oven temperature for this recipe. If you use a higher temperature, the cake will turn brown and will sink once cooled.

Low-Sugar Milk Chocolate

Homemade sugar-free milk chocolate is a great way to satisfy your inner chocoholic—without diving into unhealthy sugar and additives. Just be sure to choose milk powder that contains as little milk sugar as possible. This scaled-back recipe makes just 4 ounces (115 g) of chocolate, so double or triple the ingredients if you're planning to serve a bigger crowd.

¼ cup (30 g) milk powder

3 tablespoons (24 g) powdered erythritol

1 tablespoon (7 g) unsweetened dark cocoa powder

Pinch unrefined sea salt or Himalayan salt

2 ounces (60 g) cocoa butter

20 drops vanilla stevia

—

Yield: 8 servings

Sift the milk powder, erythritol, dark cocoa powder, and salt into a small bowl. (Sifting removes any lumps.) Set aside.

Melt the cocoa butter in a small saucepan over low heat, or in the microwave oven in thirty-second spans. Be careful not to let the cocoa butter boil. Add the cocoa butter and vanilla stevia to the cocoa powder mixture and stir well until the mixture is smooth and the erythritol has dissolved. Heat in the microwave or in a saucepan over low heat if the mixture looks grainy. Pour the mixture into preferred chocolate molds and place it in the fridge for 2 to 3 hours to set.

When done, store in the fridge in an airtight container for up to one week.

TIP:

For even lower-sugar milk chocolate (and a vegan, dairy-free version), replace the milk powder with sugar-free coconut milk powder.

NUTRITION INFO

IN TOTAL:	
14.5 G PROTEIN	
63.1 G FAT	
11.3 G NET CARBS	
670 KCAL	
PER ½ OUNCE (14 G):	
1.8 G PROTEIN	
7.9 G FAT	
1.4 G NET CARBS	
84 KCAL	

NOTE:

Don't omit the salt—it's a must. Salt adds a decadent note to the sweet chocolate and rounds out the flavors. Salt is a mandatory ingredient in just about every recipe that calls for chocolate.

One-Two-Three-Four-Five Cake

Baking a healthy, sugar-free, gluten-free cake is as easy as counting to five. Serve this small and simple-but-scrumptious cake with jam and cream, or ice it with your favorite sugar-free frosting. It's super-versatile—you can add nuts, dark chocolate chips, sugar-free jam, or flavoring to the batter for extra variation—and it makes the perfect birthday cake, too.

1 cup (115 g) almond flour

2 teaspoons aluminum-free baking powder

3 tablespoons (21 g) coconut flour

4 tablespoons (32 g) powdered erythritol

5 eggs

—

Yield: 12 to 20 servings

Preheat the oven to 350°F (175°C). Combine the almond flour, baking powder, coconut flour, and sweetener in a small bowl. Mix well to break up any lumps.

Beat the eggs until fluffy and pale, then fold in the dry ingredients. Mix with a rubber spatula until smooth. Pour the batter into a generously greased 5-inch (10 cm) cake pan. Bake for 30 minutes or until a toothpick inserted into the middle of the cake comes out clean. Remove the cake from the pan, let cool, and serve.

NUTRITION INFO

IN TOTAL:

67.9 G PROTEIN

91.2 G FAT

18.3 G NET CARBS; 1174 KCAL

PER SLICE,
IF 12 SLICES IN TOTAL:

5.7 G PROTEIN

7.6 G FAT

1.5 G NET CARBS

98 KCAL

PER SLICE,
IF 20 SLICES IN TOTAL:

3.4 G PROTEIN

4.6 G FAT

0.9 G NET CARBS

59 KCAL

Easy Fudgy Brownies

Healthy brownies—that's an oxymoron, right? Nope: These melt-in-your-mouth treats are sinfully irresistible, but they're actually good for you because they're free from grain, sugar, and artificial fats. Instead, they feature real butter, dark chocolate, and fiber-rich coconut flour for the healthiest, richest-tasting result. (Hint: These little gems taste best the day after they're made.)

1 stick (4 ounces, or 115 g) salted grass-fed butter

4 ounces (115 g) dark chocolate (minimum 85 percent cocoa solids)

¼ cup (30 g) coconut flour

2 teaspoons aluminum-free baking powder

⅓ cup (33 g) erythritol crystals

25 drops vanilla stevia

4 eggs

1 cup (115 g) chopped walnuts (optional)

—
Yield: about 12 brownies

Preheat the oven to 350°F (175 °C). Place the butter and the chocolate in a small saucepan. Place over medium heat, stirring constantly, until melted. Remove from the heat and set aside.

Combine the coconut flour and the baking powder in a small bowl. Mix well and set aside.

Combine the melted butter and chocolate mixture, erythritol crystals, and vanilla stevia in a medium bowl. Beat with an electric mixer until smooth. Add the eggs one at a time, beating well after each addition. (Don't worry if the mixture looks separated. It will become smooth after you have added all the eggs.) After adding the last egg, beat the mixture until light and fluffy, about 5 to 10 minutes. Add the coconut flour mixture and beat again until smooth. Fold in the chopped walnuts, if using.

Pour the mixture into an 8 x 8-inch (20 x 20 cm) silicone brownie pan or greased glass or ceramic baking dish. Bake for 15 to 20 minutes, or until the edges are firm but the center is still a bit wobbly. Don't overbake. Let cool completely, remove from the pan, and cut into pieces. Store in the fridge, and bring to room temperature 30 minutes before serving.

NUTRITION INFO

WALNUTS NOT INCLUDED IN THE CALCULATIONS

IN TOTAL:

50.6 G PROTEIN	
172.8 G FAT	
31.6 G NET CARBS	
1892 KCAL	

PER BROWNIE, IF 12 BROWNIES IN TOTAL:

4.2 G PROTEIN	
14.4 G FAT	
2.6 G NET CARBS	
158 KCAL	

TIP:

Add ½ cup (85 g) dark chocolate chips (with a minimum cocoa content of 85 percent) to the dough for extra-chocolaty brownies.

Crunchy One-Bowl, Five-Ingredient Cookies

It took a little trial and error, but I finally came up with a cookie recipe that my family and I love. The result? Crunchy, buttery, vanilla-flavored cookies with plenty of flavor, but no sugar, starch, or even egg. Need I say more?

1 cup (115 g) almond flour

⅓ cup (30 g) vanilla-flavored grass-fed whey protein

6 tablespoons (3 ounces, or 85 g) unsalted grass-fed butter, softened

3 tablespoons (39 g) erythritol crystals

25 drops vanilla stevia

—

Yield: about 16 cookies

Preheat the oven to 350°F (175°C). Line a baking sheet with parchment paper.

Combine all ingredients in a medium bowl. Using clean hands, knead until the mixture is well combined and the dough is smooth and free from clumps. Then shape the dough into small walnut-size balls. Place them on the lined baking sheet and flatten them with wet fingertips.

Bake for 5 to 7 minutes, or until golden brown. (Keep an eye on the cookies. They can get too brown very quickly.) Let cool completely before removing from the baking sheet. This is important because the hot cookies are very fragile. When cool, store in an airtight container in a cool, dry place for up to one week.

NUTRITION INFO

IN TOTAL:

46.7 G PROTEIN	
1321.6 G FAT	
13.9 G NET CARBS	
1439 KCAL	

PER COOKIE, IF 16 COOKIES IN TOTAL:

2.9 G PROTEIN	
8.3 G FAT	
0.9 G NET CARBS	
90 KCAL	

TIP:

Add ⅓ cup (60 g) dark chocolate chips (with a minimum cocoa content of 85 percent) to the dough to make delicious, low-sugar chocolate chip cookies.

Flourless Four-Ingredient Peanut Butter Cake in a Mug

When I made this mug cake for my son, he proclaimed, "This is the best cake you have ever made!"— and he doesn't even like peanut butter! That endorsement pretty much says it all when it comes to this incredibly easy, single-serving cake. Make one for your kids (or yourself) the next time they beg for a sweet treat. I bet they'll agree.

3 tablespoons (48 g) unsweetened peanut butter

2 tablespoons (26 g) erythritol crystals

1 egg

¼ teaspoon aluminum-free baking powder

¼ teaspoon vanilla extract (optional)

—
Yield: 1 serving

NUTRITION INFO

IN TOTAL:

19.4 G PROTEIN	
32.6 G FAT	
5.1 G NET CARBS	
395 KCAL	

Place all ingredients into a large microwave-safe mug and mix vigorously with a spoon to form a smooth batter. Microwave on high for 1 minute and 30 seconds. Check the cake after 1 minute and adjust the overall cooking time according to your microwave oven. Don't overbake. Let cool until warm and serve.

VARIATION: It's easy to vary this one-mug wonder. For peanut butter and chocolate chip cake, add 2 tablespoons (22 g) dark chocolate chips or chopped homemade sugar-free chocolate to the batter and mix well. For a peanut-butter-and-jelly cake, drop 1 tablespoon (15 g) Easy Sugar-Free Strawberry Jam (page 21) into the batter before baking. Use a fork to create a swirl in the batter, then bake.

Sugar-Free Natural-Ingredient Gummy Bears

Bursting with brisk citrus flavors, these candies have only natural ingredients, and they contain super-healthy gelatin. That makes them a far cry from the industrially produced store-bought versions. Don't worry if the hot liquid mixture doesn't seem like a lot: It makes a whopping five dozen gummy bears which your kids can enjoy to their hearts' content.

¼ **cup (60 ml) freshly squeezed orange juice**

¼ **cup (32 g) powdered erythritol**

2 **tablespoons (28 ml) freshly squeezed lemon juice**

20 **drops lemon stevia**

3 **tablespoons (21 g) gelatin powder**

2 **drops 100 percent orange essential oil**

—

Yield: about 60 gummy bears

Place all ingredients in a small saucepan and heat over medium-high heat, stirring constantly. When the gelatin has melted but the mixture is not yet boiling, remove the saucepan from the heat. Pour the liquid into a silicone gummy bear mold. (There are special bottles for this purpose on the market to make the process easier and less messy. Use one of these, if you like.) Place the mold in the refrigerator for 1 to 2 hours, remove the gummy bears from the mold, and store in an airtight container in the fridge for up to one week.

TIP:

Try different pure fruit juices in place of the orange juice, or experiment with different flavored stevia and various natural flavorings.

NUTRITION INFO

IN TOTAL:

25.9 G PROTEIN	
0.2 G FAT	
5.5 G NET CARBS	
135 KCAL	

PER GUMMY BEAR, IF 60 GUMMY BEARS IN TOTAL:

0.4 G PROTEIN	
TRACE FAT	
0.1 G NET CARBS	
2 KCAL	

NOTE:

Handle the hot candy mixture carefully, as it spills from the bottle easily.
These candies are easy to make, but unfortunately the hot liquid means that kids shouldn't help with preparation for safety reasons.

Six-Ingredient Caramel Glazed Donuts

Break out the donut maker. Soft, pillowy donuts are just a few minutes away! Of course, they're grain- and sugar-free. For a decadent finish, glaze them with my Three-Ingredient Sugar-Free Caramel Glaze on page 22 after they've cooled. Then, get ready to make a second batch: Your family will gobble them up as fast as you can make them.

FOR THE DONUTS:

¼ cup (30 g) coconut flour

2 teaspoons aluminum-free baking powder

3 eggs

⅓ cup (33 g) erythritol crystals

¼ cup (60 ml) heavy cream

2 teaspoons vanilla extract

OTHER INGREDIENTS:

¼ cup (60 ml) melted grass-fed butter, for brushing the donut maker

1 batch Three-Ingredient Sugar-Free Caramel Glaze (page 22)

—

Yield: about 24 donuts

Place the coconut flour and baking powder in a small bowl. Mix well to break up any lumps. Place the rest of the ingredients for the donuts into a medium bowl and whisk well. Gradually whisk the dry ingredients into the wet.

Heat the donut maker to medium and brush each dip generously with melted butter. Fill each dip completely with batter and close the lid. Cook for 3 minutes and then open the lid carefully. (Adjust the cooking time according to your donut maker.) Remove the cooked donuts and place on a cooling rack.

Repeat the process with the rest of the batter, brushing the dips of the donut maker generously with the melted butter before pouring in the batter.

When all donuts have cooled to room temperature, prepare the Three-Ingredient Sugar-Free Caramel Glaze and let it cool to room temperature. Drizzle the glaze over the donuts and let it set. Remove the donuts from the cooling rack. Store in an airtight container in a cool, dry place for up to two days.

NUTRITION INFO

WITH GLAZE	WITHOUT GLAZE
IN TOTAL:	IN TOTAL:
38.1 G PROTEIN	30.7 G PROTEIN
206.4 G FAT	68.2 G FAT
23.2 G NET CARBS	11.5 G NET CARBS
2110 KCAL	791 KCAL
PER DONUT, IF 24 DONUTS IN TOTAL:	PER DONUT, IF 24 DONUTS IN TOTAL:
1.6 G PROTEIN	1.3 G PROTEIN
8.6 G FAT	2.8 G FAT
1.0 G NET CARBS	0.5 G NET CARBS
88 KCAL	33 KCAL

CHAPTER 7

Drinks

Brimming with sugar, additives, and colorings, store-bought soft drinks, lemonades, and iced teas are definite no-nos when you're kicking the sugar habit. Luckily, it's simple to prepare healthy, sugar-free versions of all of these and more, using clean, natural ingredients that are suitable for both kids and grownups.

Basic Sugar-Free Iced Tea

If warm summer days make you crave a pitcher of iced tea, throw out that yucky powdered stuff and try this version instead. To help you quit sugar, it's not overly sweet, but it's still plenty refreshing. Adding a pinch of baking soda to the tea while brewing guarantees a smooth taste—minus the bitterness that's typical of black tea. (Baking soda is highly alkaline, so it helps neutralize the bitter acids in black tea.) Use this recipe as a template and experiment with different types of tea and stevia flavors. I bet you'll come up with dozens of unique combinations.

1 pinch baking soda

4 bags orange pekoe or other good-quality black tea

1 cup (240 ml) boiling water

½ cup (100 g) erythritol crystals

5 cups (1.2 L) ice-cold water

¼ cup (60 ml) freshly squeezed lemon juice

40 drops lemon stevia

Ice cubes for serving

—
Yield: 6 to 8 servings

Put the baking soda into a small bowl and add the tea bags. Pour in the boiling water, add the erythritol, and mix gently. Let the tea steep for 20 minutes.

Remove the tea bags, squeezing them carefully to retain all the liquid. Discard the teabags.

Transfer the mixture to a 64-ounce (1.9 L) glass pitcher. Add the ice-cold water, lemon juice, and lemon stevia, and mix well. Adjust the taste by adding more lemon stevia or unflavored stevia, if you prefer a sweeter iced tea. Fill the pitcher with ice cubes and serve.

NUTRITION INFO

IN TOTAL:

0.4 G PROTEIN	
0.1 G FAT	
1.6 G NET CARBS	
41 KCAL	

PER SERVING,
IF 6 SERVINGS IN TOTAL:

0.1 G PROTEIN	
TRACE FAT	
0.3 G NET CARBS	
7 KCAL	

PER SERVING,
IF 8 SERVINGS IN TOTAL:

0.1 G PROTEIN	
TRACE FAT	
0.2 G NET CARBS	
5 KCAL	

TIP:

Can't find lemon stevia? Just place 2 teaspoons freshly grated lemon zest into a mesh tea ball and steep it together with the tea. Remove it along with the tea bags, and increase the amount of erythritol to ¾ cup (155 g).

Guilt-Free Lemonade

This easy, four-ingredient crowd-pleaser is relatively mild and sweet, thanks to two different sweeteners: Erythritol and stevia work especially well together, yielding the desired level of sweetness without any bitter aftertaste. Be sure to use freshly squeezed juice from organic lemons for the best taste and healthiest result here. Organic lemons always taste nicest—and, of course, they're free from potentially harmful pesticides.

1 cup (240 ml) freshly squeezed lemon juice

2 quarts (1.9 L) lukewarm water

1 cup (200 g) erythritol crystals

4 teaspoons liquid stevia, or to taste

Lemon slices for garnish (optional)

—
Yield: 6 servings

Combine all ingredients in a 3-quart (2.8 L) pitcher. Stir until the erythritol is completely dissolved. Refrigerate for a couple of hours until ice cold. Serve over ice cubes or crushed ice and lemon slices.

NUTRITION INFO

IN TOTAL:

1.7 G PROTEIN

0.5 G FAT

6.2 G NET CARBS

60 KCAL

PER SERVING,
IF 16 SERVINGS IN TOTAL:

0.1 G PROTEIN

TRACE FAT

0.4 G NET CARBS

4 KCAL

Apple Pie–Infused Water

Are you in the mood for sugar-free, calorie-free, all-natural apple pie? I thought so! This is a guilt-free liquid apple pie you can enjoy to your heart's content. It won't spike your blood sugar, as traditional sugar-laden apple pie will, and it's hydrating, too. Be sure to use Ceylon cinnamon here, and in all recipes that call for cinnamon: Unlike the more commonly used cassia, or Chinese cinnamon, it isn't toxic to the liver.

7 ounces (200 g, or about 1 large) sour apple such as Granny Smith, sliced, seeds removed

2 Ceylon cinnamon sticks

1 vanilla bean, cut into 4 pieces (first lengthwise, then crosswise)

1 teaspoon freshly grated ginger

1½ quarts (1.4 L) water

Yield: 6 servings

Place the apple slices, cinnamon sticks, and vanilla bean pieces in a 2-quart (1.9 L) pitcher. Place the grated ginger in a tea ball and close the ball tightly. Place the tea ball in the pitcher and then pour in the water. Refrigerate for at least 5 hours before serving, so that the apple and the vanilla bean have time to release their flavors. Stir gently before serving.

NUTRITION INFO

IN TOTAL:

TRACE PROTEIN	
TRACE FAT	
TRACE NET CARBS	
TRACE KCAL	

PER SERVING,
IF 6 SERVINGS IN TOTAL:

TRACE PROTEIN	
TRACE FAT	
TRACE NET CARBS	
TRACE KCAL	

TIP:

For a warmer, spicier flavor, omit the vanilla bean and add ½ teaspoon whole cloves to the tea ball together with the grated ginger.

Mighty Mint Lassi

In Indian cuisine, lassis are traditional companions for spicy food, and are usually made with yogurt, ice, sweetener, and a variety of spices, such as cumin or turmeric. And both kids and adults love this mild, creamy, cooling, sugar-free version, which is flavored with fresh mint. To make it even more refreshing, add 1 cup (150 g) of crushed ice to the other ingredients and blend well—then sit back and sip.

2 cups (480 ml) ice-cold water

7 ounces (200 g) plain, organic, full-fat Greek or Turkish yogurt

10 to 15 fresh mint leaves

10 to 15 drops liquid stevia (optional)

—
Yield: 4 servings

Simply place all ingredients in a blender jar and blend until smooth and frothy. Serve over ice cubes—as an accompaniment to spicy food, or on its own as a pick-me-up on a warm day.

NUTRITION INFO

IN TOTAL:

6.5 G PROTEIN

20.0 G FAT

7.4 G NET CARBS

239 KCAL

PER SERVING,
IF 4 SERVINGS IN TOTAL:

1.6 G PROTEIN

5.0 G

1.9 G NET CARBS

60 KCAL

Supreme Orange Creamsicle Shake

You know those creamy-citrusy ice pops you loved when you were little? Well, I've given them a low-sugar makeover, and now you and your kids can enjoy their great taste in this healthy, dairy-free shake. Add 1 cup (150 g) crushed ice for extra cooling power and an especially slushy result. As it's a drink and a dessert all in one, it's the perfect way to end a light summer meal.

¼ cup (60 g) Low-Sugar
Orange Marmalade, page 19

¼ cup (60 ml) heavy cream
or coconut cream

1 cup (240 ml) ice-cold unsweetened
almond milk

20 drops orange stevia

2 drops 100 percent orange essential oil

Pinch of turmeric, for natural orange
color (optional)

—
Yield: 1 serving

Simply place all ingredients in a high-speed blender and blend until smooth. Serve immediately.

VARIATION: To turn this shake into a power breakfast or snack, add 1 scoop grass-fed, vanilla-flavored whey protein powder before blending.

NUTRITION INFO

IN TOTAL:

3.1 G PROTEIN

23.7 G FAT

5.2 G NET CARBS

252 KCAL

TIP:

Replace the Low-Sugar Orange Marmalade with Easy Sugar-Free Strawberry Jam (page 21), omit the orange essential oil, and sweeten with vanilla stevia instead of orange stevia, and *voila!*—you've got a low-sugar strawberry shake.

Creamy No-Sugar Hot Chocolate

Next time you or one of your kids need a mug of something hot, sweet, and comforting, try this nutritious version of traditional hot chocolate. Since it's sugar-free, it won't wreak havoc on your blood sugar, and the dark cocoa powder delivers a healthy hit of minerals, including iron, copper, magnesium, and potassium. It's best served with an ample amount of whipped cream and dark chocolate shavings, but if you don't tolerate dairy, it's easy to make a dairy-free version by using thick coconut cream—preservative-free, if possible—instead.

¾ cup (180 ml) boiling water

2 tablespoons (28 ml) heavy cream or coconut cream

1 tablespoon (7 g) unsweetened dark cocoa powder

10 drops vanilla stevia, or to taste

—
Yield: 1 serving

Combine all the ingredients in a large mug until well mixed. Top with whipped cream and chocolate shavings, if desired.

NUTRITION INFO

IN TOTAL:

2.0 G PROTEIN

12.0 G FAT

1.5 G NET CARBS

122 KCAL

Healthy PSL (Pumpkin Spice Latte)

Forget those artificially flavored, carb-laden pumpkin spice lattes: They don't contain real pumpkin at all! This healthy version, on the other hand, does. Plus, it not only tastes wonderful, it also nourishes you from head to toe, thanks to the cream and coconut oil, both of which contain healthy fats. Better yet, this easy drink hardly takes more than sixty seconds to make—just mix all ingredients together and enjoy.

¾ cup (180 ml) boiling water

¼ cup (60 g) 100 percent
pure pureed pumpkin

2 tablespoons (28 ml) heavy cream
or coconut cream

1 tablespoon (14 g) extra-virgin
coconut oil

1 to 2 teaspoons instant espresso
powder

½ teaspoon pumpkin pie spice

10 drops vanilla stevia, or to taste

Whipped cream, for garnish (optional)

—
Yield: 1 serving

Combine all the ingredients in a large mug and stir until well mixed. (Use an immersion blender for best results, but be careful not to burn yourself when handling hot drinks!) Top with whipped cream, if desired, and serve immediately.

NUTRITION INFO

IN TOTAL:

1.2 G PROTEIN

25.5 G FAT

4.5 G NET CARBS

265 KCAL

Rich Sugar-Free Eggnog

Ready for the ultimate eggnog eggsperience? This velvety, mousse-like eggnog is sure to be memorable. Because regular milk contains milk sugar, I use carb-free unsweetened almond milk. Thanks to its rich texture and delicate, lingering taste, you won't miss the milk one bit.

4 eggs, separated*

½ cup (65 g) powdered erythritol

25 drops vanilla stevia, or to taste

1 cup (240 ml) unsweetened almond milk

1 cup plus ½ cup (240 ml plus 120 ml) heavy cream, divided

⅓ cup (80 ml) bourbon whiskey or dark rum (optional)

Freshly grated nutmeg, for serving

—
Yield: 8 servings

NOTE

This recipe contains raw egg white. See the tip for making an egg-free version.

Place the egg yolks, erythritol, vanilla stevia, almond milk, and 1 cup (240 ml) of the heavy cream into a large saucepan. Heat over medium heat, whisking constantly, until the mixture thickens. When it is about to boil, remove it from the heat. Stir in the alcohol, if using. Let cool to room temperature and then refrigerate until cold, about 4 hours.

Meanwhile, place the egg whites into a deep, narrow bowl. Beat until soft peaks form. Set aside.

Place the remaining ½ cup (120 ml) of cream into a clean bowl. Beat until soft peaks form.

Remove the chilled custard from the fridge. Add the beaten egg whites and the whipped heavy cream and whisk until smooth. Refrigerate the eggnog for 1 hour before serving.

When you're ready to serve, whisk the eggnog well, pour it into glasses, and grate a little fresh nutmeg on top. Serve immediately.

TIP:

Don't like your eggnog too thick?
Worried about serving raw eggs?
Just leave out the beaten egg whites.

NUTRITION INFO

IN TOTAL:	
38.9 G PROTEIN	
152.9 G FAT	
11.8 G NET CARBS	
1760 KCAL	

PER SERVING, IF 8 SERVINGS IN TOTAL:	
4.9 G PROTEIN	
19.1 G FAT	
1.5 G NET CARBS	
220 KCAL	

References

Associated Press. "Truvia maker settles Hawaii-based suit for $61 million." December 5, 2014. www.hawaiinewsnow.com/story/27558493/truvia-maker-settles-hawaii-based-suit-for-61m.

Authority Nutrition: An Evidence-Based Approach. https://authoritynutrition.com. Accessed March 9, 2017. (site discontinued)

Avena, Nicole M., Pedro Rada, and Bartley G. Hoebel. "Evidence for sugar addiction: Behavioral and neurochemical effects of intermittent, excessive sugar intake." *Neuroscience and Biobehavioral Reviews* 2008 32(1): 20–39.

Birketvedt, GS, M. Shimshi, T. Erling *et al.* "Experiences with three different fiber supplements in weight reduction." *Medical Science Monitor* 2005 Jan; 11(1): 5–8.

Harcombe, Zoë. "Dr. Zoë Harcombe, Ph.D." www.zoeharcombe.com. Accessed March 9, 2017.

Kolp Institute. "Sugar: The Bitter Truth." http://kolpinstitute.org/facts-about-sugar. Accessed March 9, 2017. (site discontinued)

Lapis, Trina J, Michael H. Penner, and Juyun Lim. "Humans can taste glucose oligomers independent of the hT1R2/hT1R3 sweet taste receptor." *Chemical Senses* (2016) 41 (9): 755–762

Oklahoma Medical Research Foundation Staff. "New company explores novel therapeutic uses for aspartame." https://omrf.org/2004/08/27/new-company-explores-novel-therapeutic-uses-for-aspartame. 2004.

Rinella, Mary E. "Nonalcoholic fatty liver disease: a systematic review." *JAMA: Journal of the American Medical Association*. 2015;313(22): 2263–2273.

Spreadbury, Ian. "Comparison with ancestral diets suggests dense acellular carbohydrates promote an inflammatory microbiota, and may be the primary dietary cause of leptin resistance and obesity." *Diabetes, Metabolic Syndrome and Obesity: Targets and Therapy.* 2012; 5: 175–189.

Stanhope, Kimber L., Jean Marc Schwarz, Nancy L. Keim, *et al*. "Consuming fructose-sweetened, not glucose-sweetened, beverages increases visceral adiposity and lipids and decreases insulin sensitivity in overweight/obese humans." *The Journal of Clinical Investigation* 2009 119(5): 1322–1334.

U. S. Department of Agriculture. "Sugar and Sweeteners Yearbook Table." www.ers.usda.gov/data-products/sugar-and-sweeteners-yearbook-tables.aspx. Accessed March 9, 2017.

WebMD. "The Truth on Artificial Sweeteners." www.webmd.com/food-recipes/features/truth-artificial-sweeteners#1. 2002. (site discontinued)

Yang, Quanhe, Zefeng Zhang, and Edward W Gregg. "Added Sugar Intake and Cardiovascular Diseases Mortality Among US Adults." *JAMA Internal Medicine* 2014 174(4): 516–524.

About the Author

Elviira Krebber, a Finnish blogger and photographer, is the creator of the popular *Low-Carb, So Simple* blog, which features easy and innovative sugar-free recipes with five ingredients or less that are suitable for a gluten-free, clean eating lifestyle. More than a decade ago, she healed herself with a gluten-free, low-sugar diet, and has been an avid promoter of a starch-free, low-sugar lifestyle ever since. She is currently studying to be a nutrition therapist. She is also the author of several eBooks and a printed book in Finnish, called *Healing Ketosis—Get Healthy with Gluten-Free, Sugar-Free Food*. She speaks about ketogenic and low-sugar lifestyle both nationally and internationally.

Index